ABC of
Child Protection

Fourth Edition

ABC series

The revised and updated ABC series – written by specialists for non-specialists

- With over 40 titles, this extensive series provides a quick and dependable reference on a broad range of topics in all the major specialities

- An easy-to-use resource, covering the symptoms, investigations, treatment and management of conditions presenting in your day-to-day practice

- Full colour photographs and illustrations aid diagnosis and patient understanding of a condition

- Each book in the new series now offers links to further information and articles, and a new dedicated website provides even more support

- A highly illustrated, informative and practical source of knowledge for GPs, GP registrars, junior doctors, doctors in training and those in primary care

For further information on the entire ABC series, please visit:

www.abcbookseries.com

ABC of Ear, Nose and Throat
FIFTH EDITION
Edited by Harold Ludman and Patrick J Bradley

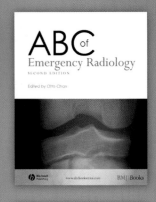

ABC of Emergency Radiology
SECOND EDITION
Edited by Otto Chan

ABC of Patient Safety
Edited by John Sandars and Gary Cook

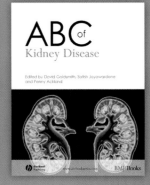

ABC of Kidney Disease
Edited by David Goldsmith, Satish Jayawardene and Penny Ackland

ABC of Clinical Haematology
THIRD EDITION
Edited by Drew Provan

ABC of Obesity
Edited by Naveed Sattar and Michael E Lean

Blackwell Publishing

BMJ|Books

ABC of

Child Protection

Fourth Edition

EDITED BY

Sir Roy Meadow
Emeritus Professor of Paediatrics and Child Health
University of Leeds, Leeds, UK

Jacqueline Mok
Consultant Paediatrician
Royal Hospital for Sick Children, Edinburgh, UK

Donna Rosenberg
Forensic Paediatrician
University of Colorado School of Medicine, Denver, CO, USA

Blackwell Publishing

BMJ|Books

© 2007 by Blackwell Publishing Ltd
BMJ Books is an imprint of the BMJ Publishing Group Limited, used under licence

Blackwell Publishing, Inc., 350 Main Street, Malden, Massachusetts 02148-5020, USA
Blackwell Publishing Ltd, 9600 Garsington Road, Oxford OX4 2DQ, UK
Blackwell Publishing Asia Pty Ltd, 550 Swanston Street, Carlton, Victoria 3053, Australia

The right of the Author to be identified as the Author of this Work has been asserted in
accordance with the Copyright, Designs and Patents Act 1988.

First edition 1989
Second edition 1993
Third edition 1997
Fourth edition 2007

1 2007

Library of Congress Cataloging-in-Publication Data
ABC of child protection / edited by Sir Roy Meadow, Jacqueline Mok,
Donna Rosenberg. -- 4th ed.
        p. ; cm.
    Rev. ed. of: ABC of child abuse / edited by Roy Meadow. 1997.
    Includes bibliographical references and index.
    ISBN 978-0-7279-1817-8 (alk. paper)
  1. Community health services for children. 2. Child health services.
3. Social work with children. 4. Child abuse. 5. Child welfare. I.
Meadow, S. R. II. Mok, Jacqueline Y. Q. III. Rosenberg, Donna, MD. IV.
ABC of child abuse.
    [DNLM: 1. Child Abuse--diagnosis--Great Britain--Legislation. 2.
Child Abuse--Great Britain--Legislation. WA 320 A1346 2007]

    RJ102.A23444 2007
    362.76--dc22

                                                    2006036144

ISBN: 978-0-7279-1817-8

A catalogue record for this title is available from the British Library

Cover image of paperchain family is courtesy of Mike Bentley and istockphoto.com

Set in 9.25/12 pt Minion by Sparks, Oxford – www.sparks.co.uk
Printed and bound in Singapore by COS Printers Pte Ltd

For further information on Blackwell Publishing, visit our website:
www.blackwellpublishing.com

Contents

Contributors

Hendrika Cantwell

Emerita professor of paediatrics, University of Colorado, Denver, CO, USA

Stephen Chapman

Consultant paediatric radiologist, Birmingham Children's Hospital, Birmingham, UK

Kenneth Feldman

Clinical professor of paediatrics, University of Washington, Seattle, WA, USA

Fiona Forbes

Consultant child and adolescent psychiatrist, Royal Hospital for Sick Children, Edinburgh, UK

Danya Glaser

Consultant child and adolescent psychiatrist, Great Ormond Street Hospital, London, UK

Christopher Hobbs

Consultant community paediatrician, St James's University Hospital, Leeds, UK

Alison Kemp

Reader in child health, Cardiff University, UK

Alex V Levin

Associate professor, departments of paediatrics, ophthalmology, and visual science, Hospital for Sick Children, University of Toronto, Canada

Roy Meadow

Emeritus professor of paediatrics and child health, University of Leeds, Leeds, UK

Russell Migita

Specialist in paediatric emergency medicine, Children's Hospital, Seattle, WA, USA

Barbara Mitchels

Children Panel solicitor and psychotherapist, Norwich, UK

Jacqueline Mok

Consultant paediatrician, Royal Hospital for Sick Children, Edinburgh, UK

Donna Rosenberg

Forensic paediatician, University of Colorado Medical School, Denver, CO, USA

Michael Preston-Shoot

Professor of social work, University of Luton, UK

Preface

When the first edition of this ABC was published, sexual abuse was reaching the headlines, and the Children Act 1989 was coming into force. Now, 18 years later, media interest and, sometimes, misconceptions continue, and a new Children Act has been published for England and Wales. Yet much has changed, there is more recorded experience, a stronger basis of evidence for detection of abuse, and clearer guidelines for those suspecting or identifying it.

This book is a text for doctors about the recognition and diagnosis of child abuse. It emphasises those aspects of the clinical history, examination, and investigation that are useful in deciding whether the child's problems are the result of natural or unnatural (abusive) causes. The medical contribution depends not only on doctors but also on nurses and other staff of the health service who deal with children and who may be the first to notice abuse or be informed of it. This book should help them. It will also be helpful to all those concerned with child protection whether from social services, the police, legal or teaching professions, in understanding the way that medical diagnosis is made and the strengths and weaknesses of medical opinions and reports. The book outlines procedures and the respective roles of those who contribute to child protection but does not go into the detail of management. For the benefit of readers who consult individual chapters, some essential information is repeated.

Our aim has been to provide a balanced view of contemporary issues. The level of knowledge is that to which a paediatrician should aspire. Regardless of their speciality interest, all paediatricians need to be knowledgeable about child abuse because of its commonness and the diversity of its presentation. For general practitioners, accident and emergency staff, and other medical specialists there should be more than enough information in this book. The further reading includes detailed reviews and important papers about commonly encountered, and contested, topics. The clinician involved should always check the recent scientific literature for additional information, and be cautious in giving undue priority to any single published study. In addition to national guidelines, there are usually local guidelines about procedures to be followed when child abuse is suspected or detected. This book should be used in conjunction with those guidelines.

Compared with the previous edition, nearly half the chapters are completely new, and the rest have had major revision. The authors include nine new contributors, representatives from different disciplines and different specialties, as well as a more international flavour, with five from USA and Canada. The new co-editors reflect those trends. Dr Jacqueline Mok is the lead clinician in child protection in Edinburgh, and Dr Donna Rosenberg, formerly director of the child protection service at Henry Kempe Center/University of Colorado Health Sciences Center, is a consulting forensic paediatrician in the United States. They bring experience, knowledge and wisdom to challenging work.

RM

CHAPTER 1

Child Abuse in Society

Roy Meadow

Table 1.1 Reason for child being on CPR

	Prevalence
Neglect	39%
Physical abuse	19%
Emotional abuse	17%
Sexual abuse	10%
Multiple	15%

Girls account for 48% of all registrations and 62% of sexual abuse registrations

This year most departments of social services will be notified of more than 20 times as many cases of suspected child abuse as they were 30 years ago. Although many of the reports will prove to be unfounded, the common experience is that proved cases of child abuse are four or five times as common as they were. Over 32 000 children in the UK are listed on child protection registers (Box 1.1, Table 1.1). This poses enormous burdens on staff in the health and social services and raises many problems about the lives and welfare of children in our society. Determining whether there is a true increase of child abuse or whether the figures merely reflect increased awareness rests to some extent on the definition of child abuse.

What is child abuse?

A child is considered abused if he or she is treated in a way that is unacceptable in a given culture at a given time. The last two clauses are important because children are treated differently not only in different countries but within a multicultural country; and even within a city, there are subcultures of behaviour and variations of opinion about what constitutes abuse of children. Moreover, standards change over the years as the public perception of the thresholds for abuse change: corporal punishment has become much less acceptable in the past 10 years. Legislation follows, and sometimes leads,

---

Box 1.1 **Child protection registers (CPR)**

Registration rates per 10 000 children aged <18:
- England 23
- Scotland 18
- Wales 34
Over 32 000 children in the UK are registered

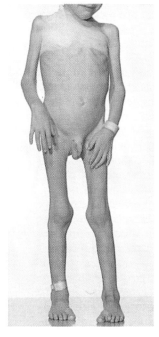

Figure 1.1 Starving.

public opinion: in Scotland it is illegal to shake a child, use an implement to hit a child, or strike a child's head during punishment.

Types of abuse (Figs 1.1–1.8)

Physical abuse (non-accidental injury)—The prototype of physical abuse—"the battered baby"—was described by Henry Kempe of Denver, Colorado, in 1962 and has been well publicised ever since. Physical abuse entails soft tissue injury to the skin, eyes, ears, and internal organs as well as to ligaments and bones. Burns and scalds are included. Most of this abuse is short term and violent, though it may be repetitive. There are subgroups with more long term persistent injury, including poisoning, suffocation, and fabricated or induced illness.

Neglect—This is failing to provide the love, care, food, or physical circumstances that will allow a child to grow and develop normally. It is also intentionally exposing a child to any kind of danger.

Sexual abuse—This occurs when dependent, developmentally immature children and adolescents participate in sexual activities

1

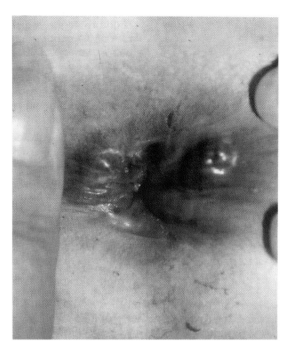

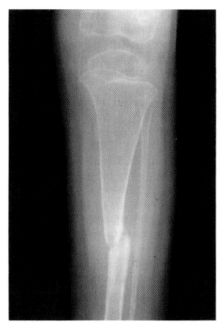

Figure 1.4 Breaking.

Figure 1.2 Buggering.

that they do not fully comprehend, to which they are unable to give informed consent, and that violate the social taboos of family roles. Such abuse ranges from inappropriate fondling and masturbation to intercourse and buggery. Children may also be forced to participate in producing pornographic photographs and videos, or be victims of abuse through the extended family network and sex rings.

Emotional abuse—This has no generally agreed definition. Some regard a child as abused if he or she has a behavioural disturbance to which the parents fail to respond appropriately in terms of modifying their behaviour or seeking professional help. Most would consider a child to be emotionally abused, however, if the child's behaviour and emotional development were severely affected by the parents' persistent neglect, rejection, or terrorisation.

Commonly, different types of abuse overlap with each other so a child may be abused in several different ways either at the same time or sequentially.

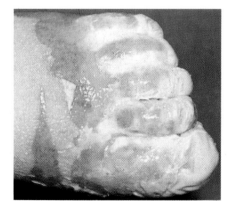

Figure 1.3 Scalding.

Most abuse occurs within the family. The adult may harm the child both actively and passively and by acts of both commission and omission. One parent may be active in beating the child, another just as harmful in failing to protect a child from the sexual advances of a cohabitant. A parent who fails to provide food or love for a child may also commit physical assault.

At least half of the abuse that occurs, sometimes over lengthy periods of the child's life, goes undisclosed at the time, even though it is known or suspected by a person or people not directly involved.

Prevalence

The online child protection resource of the National Society for the Prevention of Cruelty to Children, London, can be found at www.nspcc.org.uk/inform

Assessing the prevalence of abuse has many problems. Much depends on how abuse is defined and whether minor degrees of abuse are included. The problems of subjectivity and lack of standardisation, as well as the changing thresholds, can make historical comparisons unreliable. The National Society for the Prevention of Cruelty to Children (NSPCC) provides useful figures together with explanatory text on its website. The two most common ways of measuring abuse have been by retrospective survey of older children and adults and by quantifying the recorded activity of the agencies and services dealing with abused children. Both methods have big limitations, particularly the latter, which depends so much on the readiness of the professionals to recognise abuse and on the sociolegal structure to deal with it.

A recent survey of young adults in the UK by May-Chahal and colleagues found that, though more than 90% said that they came from a warm and loving background, maltreatment was experienced by 16% of the total sample. Serious maltreatment included 7% physical abuse, 6% emotional abuse, 6% absence of care, and

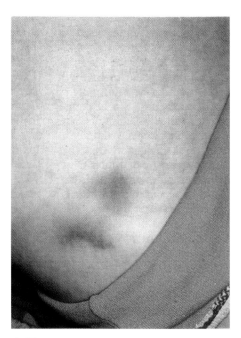

Figure 1.5 Pinching.

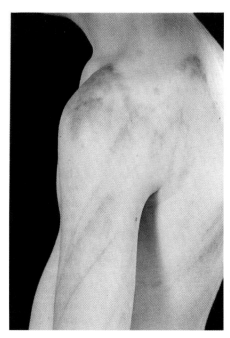

Figure 1.6 Lashing.

11% contact sexual abuse. Four per cent of children up to the age of 12 are brought to the notice of professional agencies (social service departments or the NSPCC) because of suspected abuse. Some of that abuse is not proved and some of it is mild, but a UK survey has shown that each year at least one child in 1000 under the age of 4 experiences severe physical abuse—for example, fractures, brain haemorrhage, or severe internal injuries.

Information from child protection registers is a useful measurement of professional activity but is a proxy measure of abuse. Children are registered only if they are at risk; if the abuser has moved from the household the child is not registered. As many children are de-registered each year as registered. The differences in registration rates for different parts of the UK are more likely to reflect child protection practices than large differences in the occurrence of abuse. Neglect is the most common reason for registration. One fifth of all children registered are being "looked after" by their local authority, most as a result of care orders. The figures for "looked after" children are likely to be one of the more meaningful indices of child abuse. In recent years in the United Kingdom about 60 per 10 000 children have been looked after.

Mortality rates are uncertain, partly because many cases may be undetected. Criminal statistics are of limited use, tending more to reflect detection skills and prosecution practice. In 2003, UNICEF reported that child maltreatment death rates in rich nations ranged from 0.1 to 2.2 per 100 000 children (see Jenny 2006 and UNICEF 2003).

It is difficult to know if child abuse is increasing or decreasing and equally difficult to suggest why it should. Increased awareness, better professional recognition, and unwillingness by society to tolerate the abuse of children, however, have a major impact on epidemiological statistics.

Though the thresholds for defining child abuse have moved steadily lower, professionals have become more mindful of the potentially damaging effects of overzealous intervention. Similarly, they are wary of removing children from their families because of the fear that the state is not necessarily a better parent than an abusing or inadequate biological parent.

Aetiology

Both boys and girls are abused. First born children are more often affected, and within a family sometimes just one of several children is abused. Young children are most at risk, partly because they are more vulnerable and partly because they cannot seek help elsewhere. Children aged under 2 are most at risk from severe physical abuse. Death from abuse is rare after the age of 1 (see chapter 10 and Wilczynski 1997).

The child's parents or cohabitants living in the home carry out most abuse. Young parents are more likely to abuse than older ones. It is common for both parents to be involved with physical abuse and neglect; sex abuse is more commonly perpetrated by men, while poisoning, suffocation, and fabricated or induced illness are usually

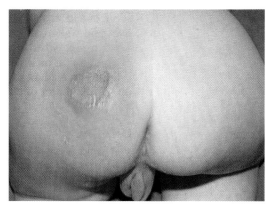

Figure 1.7 Burning.

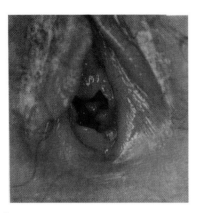

Figure 1.8 Raping.

perpetrated by the mother. Abusing parents usually do not have an identified mental illness, though many show personality traits predisposing to violent behaviour or inappropriate sexual behaviour. Child abuse is more likely in those who are socially deprived and in unstable families without a wage earner, but it is important to recognise that it occurs in all layers of society. Parental stress, domestic violence, and drug and alcohol misuse are common background factors.

Though there is a tendency for those who were abused to abuse their own children, more than a third of mothers abused as children nevertheless provide good care for their children and do not abuse them.

There is increasing concern from paediatric and social workers, but a shortage of reliable evidence, about the frequency and variety of abuse incurred by disabled children or in the families of refugees and asylum seekers, as well as a lack of comparative data for different ethnic groups. Such children tend to be in a vulnerable population, likely to be misunderstood by others.

Outcome

Recurrence of abuse is common: with a risk of 17% for physical abuse and even higher for neglect. A study in Wales (Sibert JR, et al. 2002) found that 30% of infants returned to their families after abuse were abused again. Recurrently abused children have increasingly worse outcomes. Many studies have followed abused and neglected children into early adulthood. They are at increased risk of physical and mental illness, delinquency, homelessness, unhealthy lifestyles, and violence. A renewed cycle of abuse is common when they become parents.

Awareness of the commonness of child abuse is an important step towards its recognition. The other necessary requirement is for doctors and nurses to be aware of the variety of ways in which children are abused. Many normal people comprehend the way in which a weary parent strikes an exasperating child but many normal people are too decent to imagine the degree of depravity, violence, cruelty, and cunning associated with child abuse. It is necessary to be aware of these wider limits because we can recognise and manage disorders only if we know about them from either experience or teaching. The chapters that follow will deal with both the common and the less common forms of child abuse.

Further reading

Cawson P, Wattam C, Brooker S, Kelly G. *Child maltreatment in the UK: a study of the prevalence of child abuse and neglect.* London: NSPCC 2000.

Department for Education and Skills. 2004 *Statistics of education: children looked after by local authorities.* London, DfES, 2004.

Jenny C, Isaac R. The relation between child death and child maltreatment. *Arch Dis Child* 2006;91:265–9.

Kempe CH, Silverman FN, Steele BF, Droegemueller W, Silver HK. The battered-child syndrome. *JAMA* 1962;181:17–24.

May-Chahal C, Cawson P. Measuring child maltreatment in the United Kingdom. *Child Abuse Neglect* 2005;29:969–84.

Sibert JR, Payne EH, Kemp AM, Barber M, Rolfe K, Margan RJ, et al. The incidence of severe physical child abuse in Wales. *Child Abuse Neglect* 2002;26:267–76.

Wilczynski A. *Child homicide.* Glasgow: Bell and Bain, 1997.

Hindley N, Ramchandani PG, Jones DPH. Risk factors for recurrence of maltreatment: a systematic review. *Arch Dis Child* 2006;91:744–52.

CHAPTER 2

Non-accidental Injury: The Approach

Alison Kemp, Jacqueline Mok

Physical abuse is the most common category of non-accidental injury (NAI). Typical injuries include bruises, lacerations, bites, burns, and scalds, the commonest of which are bruises, occurring in up to 80% of physically abused children.

All practitioners must be aware of the features of non-accidental injury (Box 2.1) and apply the same diagnostic rigor as they do in other clinical situations. It may be the only time that a child from an abusing environment presents with signs of physical abuse, giving the health professional a chance to make the diagnosis and start the child protection process. If the diagnosis is missed, so is the opportunity to protect the child from further or more serious abuse. Equally, if an incorrect diagnosis of child abuse is made, the consequences for the family will be devastating.

Assessing a child when non-accidental injury is suspected

A concerned adult outside the immediate family circle, such as a teacher, health visitor, neighbour, or relative, may bring the child to the attention of the doctor. The child with their parent may present to primary care services, accident and emergency, or acute paediatric teams with a history of an incident that does not explain the injury seen. Child abuse is rarely an isolated event and evidence of other types of abuse or previous injury should be looked for. The medical information forms only one piece of the jigsaw, and all doctors should be aware of and follow local and national guidance on inter-agency working (see Fig. 2.1 for pathway).

When non-accidental injury is suspected, the role of the doctor is to perform a comprehensive paediatric assessment, with the same systematic and rigorous manner as would be appropriate to the investigation and management of any other potentially fatal condi-

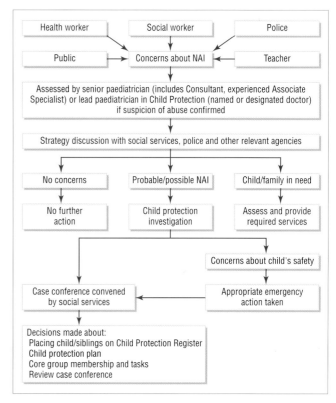

Figure 2.1 Referral pathway for cases of suspected non-accidental injury.

tion. The "whole child" must be assessed, including other medical problems, growth and development, and educational, family, and social history (Box 2.2). The risks to other children in the household must be considered. The findings must be carefully documented as they may be required for civil or criminal court hearings at a later date.

Everyone has a responsibility to protect children. Less experienced practitioners must be aware of the possibility of non-accidental injury but must also accept the limit of their responsibility and seek further guidance from the consultant paediatrician on call or the lead paediatrician (named or designated doctor) for child protection. The doctor must be objective and remember that the child's safety and welfare are paramount. Paediatric assessments should be carried out only by those trained to do so, either by consultant paediatricians or under their supervision. Where detailed forensic evidence is required, the paediatrician should seek the assistance of a forensic medical examiner to interpret injuries and collect necessary specimens (Fig. 2.2). Bite marks are best assessed with the help of a forensic dentist.

The child protection register should be checked by telephoning social services, and local as well as national guidelines should be followed to ensure the safety of the child (see chapter 20). Social services have a statutory responsibility to make enquiries when concerns are expressed about a child, while police have a duty to investigate. A concern is a starting point to look and think further. The doctor should try to discuss his or her concerns with the parents, unless to do so would place the child at risk of further harm or jeopardise enquiries. All cases of suspected non-accidental injury should be subject to a strategy discussion between professionals from health services, social services, the police, and other relevant agencies. If a

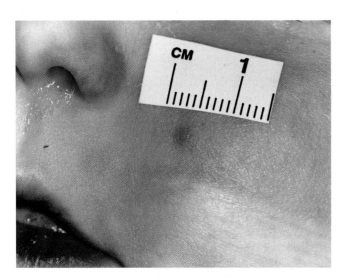

Figure 2.2 A lesion photographed and recorded with measurement during an examination.

referral is made to social services by telephone, this should be confirmed in writing within 48 hours. Failure to refer a child with suspected non-accidental injury might be considered a breach of duty which could lead to, say, a claim by the child of clinical negligence. In many countries, reporting suspected child abuse is mandatory, and failure to do so is a punishable offence.

History

A detailed description of the dynamics of causation will help the clinician to judge whether the explanation fits the injury sustained. Older children may give explanations for injuries themselves. They must be given the opportunity to do so but care must be taken that these are independent of adult coercion or intimidation. The child may disclose information during the course of assessment once they have built up confidence in and a relationship with members of the child protection team. The child's explanations, views, and wishes must be considered carefully throughout the process.

Examination

The older child should be given the option of being seen alone, without a parent present. It is wise to have a chaperone during the examination; parents may not be the appropriate chaperones. The doctor should document any observations made during the examination. These include the interaction between parent and child, the state of clothing, and unusual or inappropriate behaviours in the child (anxiously caring for the parent or overfriendly with strangers). Normal healthy features in the child should also be documented: happiness, playfulness, and confidence.

During the examination the doctor should identify the full extent of injury; check the general health, growth and development, state of nutrition, and general care that the child is receiving; and exclude signs of associated or confounding clinical illness. When a child is assessed, all areas of the skin and body must be examined, and each visible injury should be measured carefully, described, and documented on a body chart. Photographs are highly recommended to record the site, size, extent, and appearance of the injury for purposes of evidence and second opinion. All photo-documentation must be recorded according to national standards of consent and data protection, as well as ensuring that a chain of evidence is preserved.

Further reading

Department of Health. *What to do if you're worried a child is being abused.* London: Department of Health, 2003. www.dh.gov.uk/assetRoot/04/06/13/ 03/04061303.pdf

Lord Laming. The Victoria Climbié inquiry, 2003. www.victoria-climbie-inquiry .org.uk/finreport/downloadreport.htm

Royal College of Paediatrics and Child Health. Child protection companion. London: RCPCH, 2006.

CHAPTER 3

Bruises

Alison Kemp, Jacqueline Mok

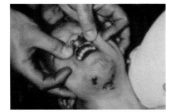

Figure 3.1 Torn frenum.

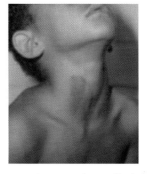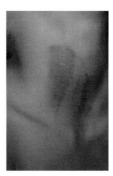

Figure 3.3 Bruises on neck caused by belt.

The key question that the clinician must address is whether bruises have been sustained after an unintentional injury or whether they have been inflicted (Box 3.1). The published evidence base in this field is modest, but sufficient to inform this decision.

Bruises from accidents

Most children sustain bruises from everyday bumps and falls, and the number that a child sustains increases with mobility. Bruises in a non-mobile baby of less than 6 months of age who has not been abused are very uncommon. On the other hand, most children 2 years and upwards will have one or more bruises at any one time.

Unintentional bruises characteristically occur on the front of the body, and up to 90% are over bony prominences. The commonest sites in ambulant children are the knees and shins. Toddlers who

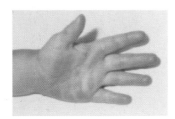

Figure 3.2 Marks on palm caused by belt.

are cruising and starting to pull themselves up to standing sustain bruises to their head; these are found on the forehead or over cheek bones where children have knocked into obstacles or low furniture.

Bruises in physical abuse

In contrast, bruises sustained from physical abuse can be seen anywhere on the body (Figs 3.1–3.9, 3.11). The commonest sites are the head and neck followed by the buttocks, back, upper arms, and abdomen. These regions are relatively protected in knocks or falls but are vulnerable to a strike from an abusing adult. Bruising on the face, ears, or neck, or clusters of bruises and multiple bruises over several sites are of particular concern.

Bruises that carry the imprint of an implement used are highly suggestive of physical abuse. Petechiae confined to the head and neck may suggest an asphyxial injury, in the absence of an explanation (history of severe coughing, prolonged vomiting or crying, signs of a viral illness). Linear or multiple bruises of similar shape over the same anatomical area or the trunk and adjacent limb need careful consideration in light of the explanation given and again suggests physical abuse.

Box 3.1 **Prevalence of unintentional bruising in children by age**

- 0–6 months <1%
- 6–12 months 10–12%
- 12–24 months 40–50%
- 24–35 months 60–80%
- Primary school children 60–80%

Figure 3.4 Bristle marks on forehead of child beaten with hairbrush.

Can you age a bruise?

Practitioners are often asked to give an estimate of the age of a bruise. This is usually at the request of the police or legal professional who want to eliminate or include possible perpetrators in their inquiries. Current literature suggests that it is inappropriate to attempt precise timing of injury.

Many paediatricians attempt to age a bruise from its colour. Different people heal at different rates, however, as do bruises on different parts of the body heal.

Factors that will affect the colour of a bruise are:

- Force of injury
- Depth of bruising—deep and superficial bruises sustained at the same time may be of different colours
- Site of the bruise—blood tracking down from an injury sustained earlier can appear at another site later
- Skin colour of the child—bruises are easier to see on light skinned children.

Clinicians are poor at discriminating colours accurately either in vivo or from photographs. With these factors in mind it is important to review the science and evidence on which we base an estimate of the age of a bruise.

Histology textbooks and recent publications report the general colour trend of a bruise from red/purple/blue in an acute bruise to yellow/green/brown as it heals. The time interval for this resolution is variable, however, and a bruise may resolve without going through this colour progression. Different colours can be seen in a bruise at any one time. Colours in a bruise come and go. Bruises sustained at the same time can have a different colour.

Red has been associated traditionally with recent bruises, but red has also been reported in bruises up to a week old (Fig. 3.5). Blue, brown, grey, and purple colours have been reported in bruises up to 14 days old. While yellow has been associated with older resolving bruises, it has also been reported in bruises less than 48 hours old. Therefore it is unwise to give an exact timescale for the causation of a bruise.

Figure 3.5 Red bruises are not always recent.

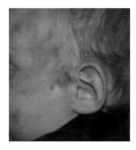

Figure 3.6 Slap mark.

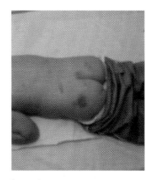

Figure 3.7 Bruises on buttocks.

If a bruise is associated with a laceration, common sense suggests that if there is active bleeding, the injury is new. An injury that shows granulation scab formation is older and likely to have occurred within days or weeks, and one that has healed and left a scar can be many months or years old.

Investigations

A child under 2 years who has bruises that are suspected to have arisen from physical abuse should have a skeletal survey x ray investigation to exclude occult fractures. Infants and young babies are vulnerable to serious and life threatening abuse that may present with relatively mild symptoms. All infants with suspected non-accidental injury should have their eyes examined to exclude retinal haemorrhages and careful consideration should be given as to whether cranial neuro-imaging is indicated to exclude the presence of non-accidental head injury.

Bruising is a common symptom of both physical abuse and bleeding disorders. Bleeding disorders, however, present with a minimal

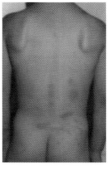

Figure 3.8 Bruises of different ages on lower back.

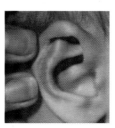

Figure 3.9 Bruising of the pinna.

or absent history of trauma, bruising or bleeding that is out of proportion to the injury received, unusual patterns of bleeding or bruising, and, sometimes, associated signs of the disorder. It must also be remembered that children who have bleeding diathesis sometimes also experience physical abuse. Therefore the patterns of bruising must be assessed carefully.

Initial investigations to exclude a major bleeding diathesis should include a full blood count and blood film as well as a coagulation screen that includes a prothrombin time (PT), activated partial thromboplastin time (aPTT), fibrinogen concentration, and thrombin time (TT). Measurement of factor VIII and factor IX and von Willebrand factor antigen and activity is also recommended in all cases of suspected NAI as a normal or marginally prolonged aPTT can be associated with a significant decrease in factor VIII or IX concentrations or with von Willebrand disease.

Conditions that mimic bruises

Several conditions may be confused with bruising in physical abuse. Most, however, have associated patterns of clinical signs and symptoms or can be directly excluded with appropriate investigations.

Bites

Human bites are reported in physical abuse. The typical appearance is that of a 2–5 cm oval or circular bruise or laceration, made by two opposing concave arcs of the perpetrator's teeth (Fig. 3.10). There may be associated central bruising. Traditionally measurement of the intercanine distance of the bite will distinguish adult bites (where the measurement is 3–4.5 cm) from that of a child (where the distance is <2.5 cm). Forensic odontologists can work to the guidelines of the British Association of Forensic Odontologists (see www. bafo.org.uk/list.php) for the analysis of bite marks, and may identify the perpetrator from unique dental characteristics within the bite mark. Paediatricians should ensure that accurate photographs are taken of any suspected bite using a right angled measuring device,

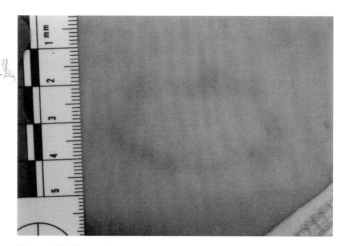

Figure 3.10 Bite mark.

Figure 3.11 Whip marks.

and taken in at least two planes if the bite is on a curved surface. An early referral should be made to a forensic dentist.

Summary

The diagnosis of non-accidental injury requires multi-agency working and should be made by an experienced paediatrician, piecing the information together in a forensic manner. An injury must never be interpreted in isolation and must always be assessed in the context of medical and social history, developmental stage, explanation given, full clinical examination, and relevant investigations. If, on the balance of probability, it is decided that non-accidental injury has occurred then the safety of the child must be ensured by a multi-agency investigation through the child protection process.

Further reading

Bariciak ED, Plint AC, Gaboury I, Bennett S. Dating of bruises in children: an assessment of physician accuracy. *Pediatrics* 2003;112:804–7.

Labbé J, Caouette G. Recent skin injuries in normal children. *Pediatrics* 2001;108:271–6.

Maguire S, Mann M, Sibert J, Kemp A. Are there patterns of bruising in childhood which are diagnostic or suggestive of abuse? A systematic review. *Arch Dis Child* 2005;90:182–6.

Maguire S, Mann M, Sibert J, Kemp A. Can you age bruises accurately in children? A systematic review. *Arch Dis Child* 2005;90:187–9.

Munang LA, Leonard PA, Mok J. Lack of agreement on colour description between clinicians examining childhood bruising. *J Clin Forensic Med* 2002;9:171–4.

Table 3.1 Conditions that mimic bruising

Mongolian blue spot	A grey purple mark present at birth often found over the lower back or buttocks in about half of black and Asian children and in some white children
Coining/cupping	Reddish markings on the skin of children caused by traditional remedies of rubbing an ailing child with coins or placing a heated cup on the skin to aid recovery
Infection	Meningococcal septicaemia causes a disseminated non-blanching purpuric rash Cellulitis can cause a bruised appearance especially to the face
Bleeding diathesis	Defects in small blood vessels: Henoch Schonlein purpura Platelet abnormalities: idiopathic thrombocytopenia Coagulation disorders: haemophilia, von Willebrands, etc Others: leukaemia, disseminated intravascular coagulation, haemolytic uraemic syndrome

Stephenson T, Bialas Y. Estimation of the age of bruising. *Arch Dis Child* 1996;74:53–5.

Sugar NF, Taylor JA, Feldman KW. Bruises in infants and toddlers: those who don't cruise rarely bruise. Puget Sound Pediatric Network. *Arch Pediatr Adolesc Med* 1999;153:399–403.

Thomas AE. The bleeding child; is it NAI? *Arch Dis Child* 2004;89:1163–7.

Useful websites

Cardiff online information service www.core-info.cf.ac.uk

The British Association of Forensic Dentists www.bafo.org.uk/list.php

CHAPTER 4

Burns and Scalds

Christopher Hobbs

Burn and scald injuries occur in children in three distinct circumstances that relate to the pattern of care the child has received (see Box 4.1). Burns and scalds within the range of child abuse are seen as serious injuries, as sadistic and linked with the sexual or violent arousal of an adult, and as punitive measures to evoke fear ("I'll teach him a lesson").

Prevalence

Deliberately inflicted burns and scalds are found in 10% of physi-

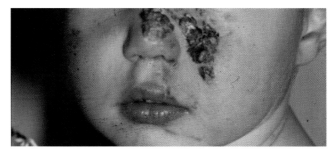

Figure 4.2 Old healing scald in 18 month old toddler. Neglect implied by delay in presentation. Presence of other injuries confirmed abuse.

Box 4.1 **Circumstance of injury**

- Unintentional: lapse in usual protection given to the child
- Neglect: inadequate or negligent parenting, failing to protect the child
- Abuse: deliberately inflicted injury

cally abused children, 5% of sexually abused children, and 1–16% of all children presenting at hospital with burns and scalds. Many cases are not recognised and not reported. In the absence of other injuries diagnosis may be difficult. The peak age for accidental burns is during the 2nd year and for abuse during the 3rd year.

Types of thermal injury

Scalds are caused by hot water – for example, in drinks, liquid food, and baths (see Figs 4.1–4.12). Scalds cause blisters and the affected skin peels in sheets and is soggy and blanched. They may have rounded margins and patterns may be modified and enhanced by clothes. Drip, pour, and splash patterns may be seen. In immersion scalds, tide marks may be identified. The depth of injury is variable and contoured.

Contact, dry burns are caused by conduction of heat from hot objects, usually metallic – for example, clothes iron or electric fire. The injury looks like a brand mark and is sharply demarcated. It often has the shape of the object that caused it. The burn is dry and tends to be of a uniform depth.

Burns from flames are caused by fires and matches and may be identified by charring and by singed hairs.

Cigarette burns leave a circular mark and a tail if the cigarette was brushed against the skin. In physical abuse the burn tends to form a crater and to scar because the injury is deep. They may be multiple.

Electrical burns are small and deep and have exit and entry points.

Friction or carpet burns occur when, for example, a child is dragged across a floor. Bony prominences are affected and the blisters are broken.

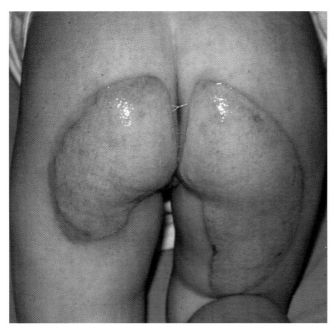

Figure 4.1 Burn from cooker hot plate. The burn was partial thickness and healed well without skin grafts. Parent claimed not to realise that the plate was hot.

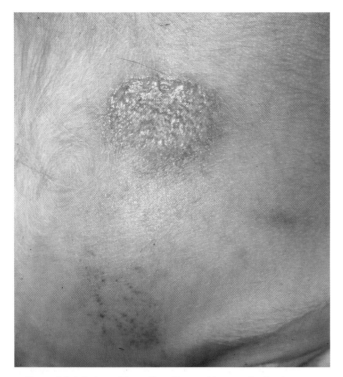

Figure 4.3 Infant aged 6 months with carpet burn on forehead.

Table 4.1 Relation between temperature and time to produce injury in adults

Temperature (°C)	Time to partial thickness burns (s)	Time to full thickness burns (s)
65	1	20
60	5	80–100
54	35	700–800
50	60	Not relevant, very long

leaves the tap is as high as 60°C, thus increasing the risks of injury to children. In 1985 the Child Accident Prevention Trust suggested that the temperature should be set at 54°C. However, under the present BS 5546 specification for the installation of gas hot water supplies for domestic purposes, the maximum temperature of the cylinder thermostat and the BS 5549 maximum for forced circulation systems are both set at 60°C. In the United States new hot water heaters are set at 48.8°C.

Transfer of heat from hot water is more predictable than in other situations – for example, contact burns from hot objects. Obviously maintenance of close contact, with air excluded, will be prevented by rapid reflex withdrawal of the part, which cannot occur in the same way with a scald. For this reason the mechanism by which contact was maintained must be ascertained in anything other than minor contact burns. Deep contact burns are likely to occur only when enforced contact has taken place. Deep burns leave permanent scars that can provide later evidence of physical abuse.

History in cases of physical abuse

Abuse should be suspected when

- The history of the burn is not consistent with the injury – for example, a 2 year old is said to have climbed into a bath of warm water, turned on the hot tap, and burnt both feet
- There is a delay in seeking treatment or treatment is avoided altogether, the injury being discovered by chance
- The parent denies that the injury is a burn when it clearly is and offers an unlikely alternative explanation
- The doctor is told that the child did it to himself or herself or that a sibling did it

Chemical burns may cause staining and scarring of the affected areas of the skin.

Radiant burns are caused by radiant energy – for example, from a fire or the sun. Injury is usually extensive and affects one aspect of an arm or leg or the body and is limited by clothing. The skin shows erythema and blistering. Such burns occur in children who are made to stand in front of a fire. Nowadays, with the ready availability of potent sun creams, severe sunburn suggests neglect.

Depth of burns and scalds

The depth of burns depends on the temperature and duration of exposure. Table 4.1 shows approximate guide times with hot water immersion for adults in thin areas of skin.

Above 60°C (140°F) children's skin burns in a quarter of the time of adult skin. In many homes the temperature of hot water as it

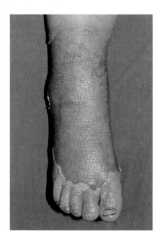

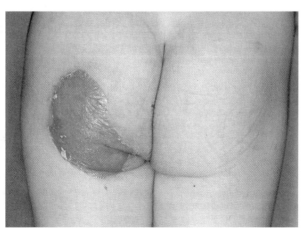

Figure 4.4 Child of 30 months with symmetrical stocking scalds (full thickness in part) to both feet and superficial scald to buttock (above) with unaffected intervening areas. History of unwitnessed bathing incident but forced immersion later admitted.

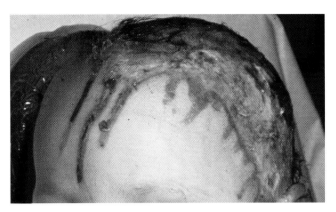

Figure 4.5 Severe burns from hot oil in 15 month old who allegedly poured the contents of a frying pan over the head. Elongated drip runs over forehead and face, showing that the injury was not consistent with the explanation.

- The incident was unwitnessed or unexplained ("I didn't see what happened, but he might have …"); in accidental injury to toddlers and young children parents are usually clear what happened, even if they did not themselves see it
- The usual consequences of injury – for example, pain – were said to be absent; the parent may say the child did not cry
- The child discloses abuse. The mother might say that the child fell over on to the fire and the child quietly tells a nurse, "Mummy did it"
- There is a history of repeated burns; for accidental burns once is usually enough for most parents and children.

Important sites and patterns

Accidental burns

Most common scalds in toddlers and older infants occur when the child pulls a kettle, pan, or cup of hot drink from a kitchen unit or table. The scald affects the face, shoulders, upper arms, and chest. Accidental scalding from falling into a hot bath leaves an irregular scald with splash marks.

Contact burns tend to be superficial, except in incidents involving electric bar fires in which the palm adheres to the bar and sustains deep destructive burns.

Burns due to physical abuse

Non-accidental burns can occur anywhere. The face and head; perineum, buttocks, and genitalia; and the hands, feet, and legs are typical sites.

Wetting and soiling may precipitate infliction of burns to the child's buttocks. Burns to the perineum and genitalia may be part of physical or sexual abuse.

Forced immersion scalds

Occur when the child or a part of the child is forcibly immersed in hot water. The face, hands, feet, buttocks, or the whole child is immersed. The child is unable to resist and is held forcibly. The characteristic pattern depends on which part is immersed – for example, hands and feet give glove and stocking patterns.

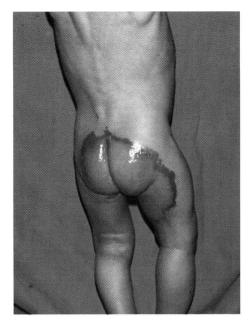

Figure 4.6 Scald to buttock caused by forced immersion.

Parts pressed on to the cooler base of the bath, sink, or container may be spared – for example, the centre of the burn may show sparing where the buttocks were pressed on the bath – the so called "hole in the doughnut" effect

Clear demarcation between burned and non-burned skin produces the tide mark. An absence of splashes indicates the child was unable to thrash around.

Hand burns

These commonly involve the dorsal surface in physical abuse, whereas in unintentional injuries – for example, from an electric fire – the palm is affected. Hands may be burned when they are held under a tap or on hot objects.

The soles of the feet may show contact or cigarette burns. Contact burns from fires (grid marks), irons, kitchen hobs, and curling tongs may also be seen on the legs and feet.

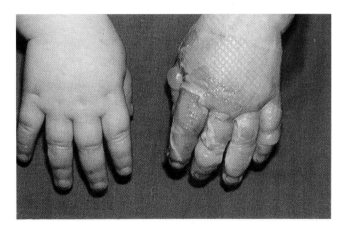

Figure 4.7 Admitted abuse in child aged 3 years, whose hand was held under the hot tap.

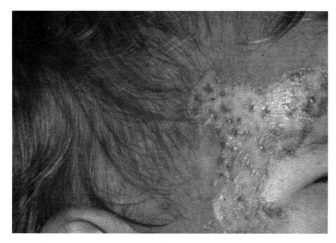

Figure 4.8 Child reported as having fallen against the fire, but the irregular roughly triangular scald was consistent with the shape of the food that family had been eating.

Characteristics of parents and children

Parents may be hostile, abusive to staff, and angry. They may refuse to allow the child to be admitted, although there is an obvious need for treatment, or threaten to discharge the child prematurely. Mothers who burn their children may be depressed, withdrawn, and seeking help and may themselves be victims of child abuse (often sexual abuse).

In contrast to parents of accidentally burned children, abusing parents may show a lack of concern for the child or a lack of guilt. Parents of accidentally burnt children may be defensive, guilty, and dislike being questioned about the cause of the injury, which should not be misinterpreted as evidence of physical abuse.

Disturbed interaction between a parent and child may show itself as anger and hostility towards the child – "It's his fault" – or as disregard of, or an inability to cope with, the child's behaviour.

Abused children may be excessively withdrawn, passive, and uncomplaining about dressings or extremely anxious, hyperactive, angry, and rebellious, especially in the children's ward. In older children a reluctance to talk about their injury and how it occurred is worrying.

Assessment

Assessment is multidisciplinary and entails the participation of doctors (general practitioner, accident and emergency doctor, plastic surgeon, and paediatrician), nurses, health visitors, social workers, police officers, and forensic scientists. In other words, the social services, the primary healthcare team, the hospital team, and the police need to liaise.

Visits to the child's home with the police may be required to inspect the bathroom, kitchen, fires, and household equipment. Temperature measurements in reproduced situations are required.

History – This must be detailed and give the exact time of the incident, the sequence of events, and the action taken. Is the child's developmental ability consistent with what he or she is said to have done? For example, could a child aged 18 months climb into a bath in the way stated?

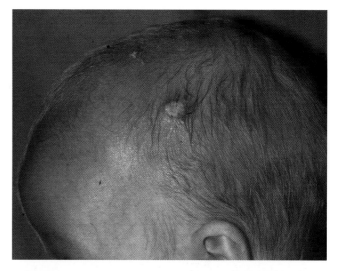

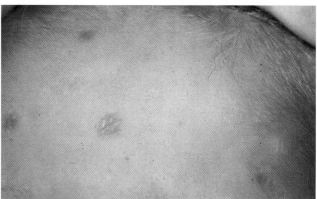

Figure 4.9 Deep cratered cigarette burn (top) on scalp of infant, said to have occurred when ash fell off parent's cigarette; cigarette burns (bottom) on forehead of older child.

Examination – Draw, measure, and photograph the injury. Manipulate the child's posture to discover the position when the injury occurred. Record the depth of the injury in relation to the temperature. Look for other injuries, and look for signs of sexual abuse during genital and anal examinations. Assess the child's demeanour, behaviour, and development. In physical abuse, failure to thrive and

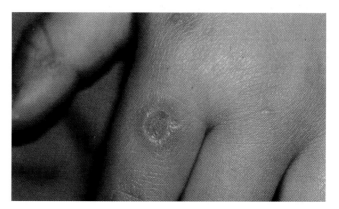

Figure 4.10 Centred deep cigarette burn on typical site on back of hand in child who also said "Mummy put her fingers in my bottom".

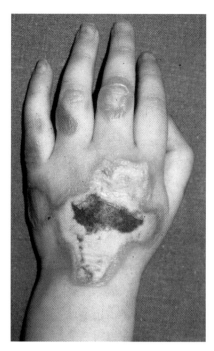

Figure 4.11 Deep burn (full thickness in part) to back of hand, which has also involved the fingers, caused by a clothes iron.

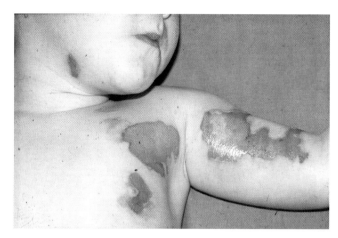

Figure 4.12 Scalds from hot drink thrown by drunken parent at 3 year old producing scattered splash effect. Differentiation from accidental scalds from pouring liquids may be difficult.

a delay in acquiring language are common. Finally, always ask the child what happened.

Differential diagnosis

When there is a lesion and no history of a burn, then skin infection or disease should be considered. Conditions that may mimic burns are:

- Epidermolysis bullosa
- Impetigo
- Papular urticaria
- Contact dermatitis
- Severe nappy rash.

Improbable accidents can occur. For example, a child could be burnt by vinegar as concentrated vinegar (glacial acetic acid) has a pH of 1.6. In addition, the buckles of seat belts or black vinyl seats heated by the sun have caused injuries that have been confused with physical abuse. In general, central heating radiators are safe but hands have been badly burnt when they have been trapped behind one, and the injudicious use of hot water bottles for babies has resulted in burns that are caused by neglect rather than abuse.

Anaesthesia, an inability to move, or congenital neurological deficit causing insensitivity to pain, syringomyelia, spina bifida, mental disability, cerebral palsy, and epilepsy may be associated with unusual burns and scalds.

Neglect should also be considered. Children left alone at home have an increased risk of dying in house fires. Fireguards should be used when there are young children in the house. Negligent parents may fail to seek treatment when their children are burnt. The effects of such neglect are serious and should also be reported to protective agencies.

Further reading

Angel C, Shu T, French D, Orihuela E. Genital and perianal burns in children: 10 years experience at a major burns center. *J Pede Surg* 2002;37:99–103.

Daria S, Sugar NF, Feldman KW, Boos SC, Benton S. Into hot water head first. Distribution of intentional and unintentional immersion burns. *Pediatr Emerg Care* 2004;20:302–10.

Feldman KW. Child abuse by burning. In: Heler RE, Kempe RS, Krugman R, eds. *The battered child*. 5th ed. Chicago: Chicago University Press, 1997.

Hobbs CJ, Wynne JM. *Physical signs of child abuse, a colour atlas*. London: WB Saunders, 2001.

Hobbs CJ. When are burns not accidental? *Arch Dis Child* 1986;61:357–61.

Scott HC, Priolo D, Cairns BA, Grany EJ, Peterson HD, Meyer AA. Return to jeopardy: the fate of paediatric burn patients who are the victims of abuse and neglect. *J Burn Care Rehab* 1998;19:367–76.

Johnson CF, Kaufman KL, Callender C. The hand as a target organ in physical abuse. *Clin Pediatr (Phila)* 1990;29:66–72.

Lenoski EF, Hunter KA. Specific patterns of inflicted burn injuries. *J Trauma* 1977;17:842.

Scalzo AJ. Burns and child maltreatment. In: Monteleone JA, Brodeur AE, eds. *Child maltreatment. A clinical guide and reference*. St Louis, MO: GW Medical, 1994.

Yeoh C, Nixon JW, Dickerson W, Kemp A, Sibert JR. Patterns of scald injuries. *Arch Dis Child* 1994;71:156–8.

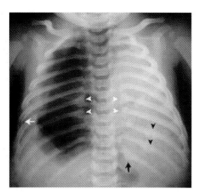

Figure 5.3 Multiple rib fractures of at least three different ages (black arrow, arrow heads, and white arrow) identified on a postmortem radiograph. Note fractures of similar ages lie directly above each other. There is a large right extrapleural haematoma associated with the freshest fracture (white arrow).

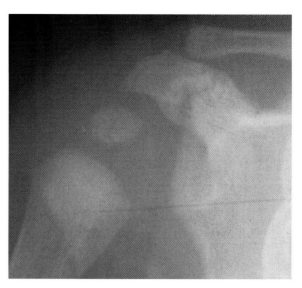

Figure 5.5 Healing fracture of the acromion.

explain posterior rib fractures. Indeed, CPR only rarely results in rib fractures in young children and those fractures usually involve the lateral or ventral aspects of the ribs.

Because the force is applied over the area of an adult's hands, the fractures usually affect similar locations on multiple adjacent ribs, usually bilaterally (Fig. 5.3). Unilateral involvement, however, occurs in about 50% of cases, and, uncommonly, there may be a single isolated rib fracture. Despite the application of a considerable compressive force, most rib fractures are clinically occult.

Rib fractures, particularly those affecting the posterior neck, may be radiographically occult before the appearance of callus. The "appearance" of healing rib fractures after a child is admitted to hospital should not automatically be interpreted as evidence that the fractures occurred in hospital; it is here that accurate dating is essential.

Long bone fractures

The morphology may suggest the mechanism of injury and this will assist the clinician in attempting to assess the truthfulness of the explanation given by the carers. A spiral fracture is the result of a

twisting force (Fig. 5.4); an oblique fracture is the result of levering (for example, lifting a child by a limb); a transverse fracture may be the result of a direct impact; a greenstick or buckle fracture will be caused by compression – for example, a fall. There is, in general, poor correlation between specific long bone fractures and the likelihood of inflicted injury, although the likelihood of an unexplained fracture being the result of abuse is greater in a child who can not yet move around independently than when he or she becomes ambulant.

Unusual fractures

Unusual fractures are the result of an unusual mechanism. The finding of a fracture that is outside one's experience of routine paediatric trauma should raise the suspicion of abuse. Examples of unusual fractures include:

- Any spinal fracture without a good accidental explanation; thoracolumbar compression fractures may occur during shaking
- Scapular fractures, the most common involves the acromion (Fig. 5.5)
- Sternum
- Pelvis
- Fingers in a non-ambulant child.

Differential diagnosis

Normal variants

There are many pitfalls in the interpretation of radiographs of the growing skeleton, and this is one of the major roles of the expert paediatric radiologist. Physiological SPNBF has already been mentioned, and there are many others, particularly affecting the metaphysis, that cause confusion.

Birth trauma

The most common fractures to occur at birth affect the clavicle, femur, and humerus. Clavicular fractures affect the middle third of the clavicle and affected babies tend to be large. Such fractures

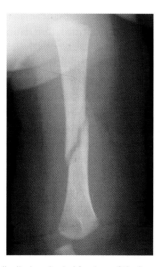

Figure 5.4 Minimally displaced spiral fracture of the humerus.

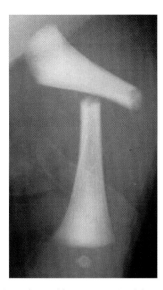

Figure 5.6 Birth injury – femoral fracture sustained during caesarean delivery.

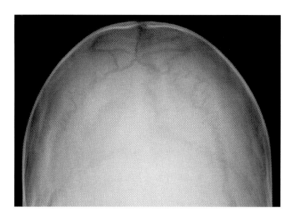

Figure 5.7 Multiple wormian bones in osteogenesis imperfecta.

usually occur when there is difficulty in delivery of the shoulder in vertex presentations and of the extended arms in breech deliveries. Femoral and humeral fractures may occur after difficult vaginal deliveries or caesarean section; any part of the bone may be affected (Fig. 5.6). Surprisingly, rib fractures occurring at birth are rare and are virtually confined to infants with birth weights above 4000 g who experience shoulder dystocia. The absence of callus 11 days or more after birth excludes a birth related injury.

Accident

This will be the commonest explanation offered for a fracture and its plausibility will rest on relating the morphology of the fracture to the mechanism of injury, radiological age to temporal history of events, and personal knowledge of and published data on common injuries at different ages. It is important to consider the developmental stage of the child – for example, a 4 week old child cannot crawl to the top of the stairs and then fall down. Falls in the domestic environment – for example, from a sofa, bed, or table – are common but do not often result in a fracture (incidence 2%). Young children more commonly injure the top half of the body because they are "top heavy." Falling down stairs is not as dangerous as might be expected. The fall on to the first step causes injuries of moderate severity, this being followed by multiple short low velocity falls. Falling down stairs while constrained in a baby walker or being held in the arms of a carer who falls down stairs, however, is far more dangerous.

Bone disease
Osteogenesis imperfecta

This inherited abnormality of quality or quantity of collagen may be confused with abuse if there is an inadequate family history and few of the other recognised signs are present, such as reduced bone density, joint laxity, blue sclera, and abnormal teeth (dentinogenesis imperfecta). Of the four main subtypes, type IV causes the greatest confusion because bone fragility is of variable severity and the

sclerae are white. Osteopenia is difficult to assess radiographically because at least 30% of bone mineral must be lost before the radiograph looks abnormal.

Wormian bones (small sutural bones in the skull) are an important sign of a congenital cause of increased bone fragility (Fig. 5.7), although it should be remembered that a few small isolated bones are common in young children and become relevant only when more than 6×4 mm in size, more than 10 in number, and arranged in a mosaic or pavement fashion. When doubt exists, the opinion of a specialist paediatrician or geneticist is helpful. Further laboratory tests that may assist are collagen analysis from fibroblast culture obtained by skin biopsy and DNA sequencing, but neither test is, at present, diagnostic and results are not available for several months.

Other conditions

These include osteopenia of prematurity, rickets, neuropathic disorders (for example, cerebral palsy and meningomyelocoele), congenital syphilis, osteomyelitis, and copper deficiency.

Further reading

British Society of Paediatric Radiology. *Draft standards for skeletal surveys in suspected non-accidental injury (NAI) in children*. www.bspr.org.uk

Carty H, Pierce A. Non-accidental injury: a retrospective analysis of a large cohort. *Eur Radiol* 2002;12:2919–25.

Chapman S, Hall CM. Non-accidental injury or brittle bones. *Pediatr Radiol* 1997;27:106–10.

Conway JJ, Collins M, Tanz RR, Radkowski MA, Anandappa E, Hernandez R, et al. The role of bone scintigraphy in detecting child abuse. *Semin Nucl Med* 1993;23:321–33.

Keats TE, Anderson MW. *Atlas of normal roentgen variants that may simulate disease.* 7th ed. St Louis: Mosby, 2001.

Kleinman PK. *Diagnostic imaging of child abuse.* 2nd ed. St. Louis, MO: Mosby, 1998.

Kleinman PK, Nimkin K, Spevak MR, Rayder SM, Madansky DL, Shelton YA, et al. Follow-up skeletal surveys in suspected child abuse. *AJR Am J Roentgenol* 1996;167:893–6.

Lonergan GJ, Baker AM, Boos SC. Child abuse: radiologic-pathologic correlation. *Radiographics* 2003;23:811–45.

Welsh Child Protection Systematic Review Group. www.core-info.cf.ac.uk

CHAPTER 6

Head Injuries

Alison Kemp, Jacqueline Mok

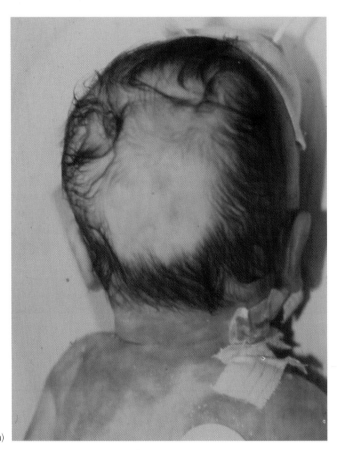

(a)

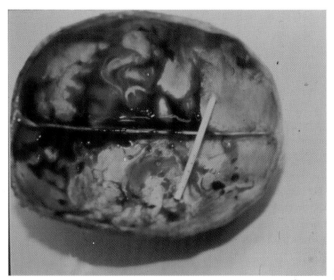

(b)

Figure 6.1 A child was brought to hospital in cardiorespiratory arrest. The parents said they had found the child "blue and not breathing." They provided no history of trauma, though bruises were found on the back of the head. Postmortem examination showed diffuse bleeding over the cerebrum.

Head injury is a serious form of physical child abuse and is responsible for the greatest number of deaths related to abuse in infancy (Fig. 6.1). Children who have sustained an inflicted injury may present with intracranial injuries but have minimal or no external injury to the head. The possibility of non-accidental injury must be considered in any infant who presents with unexplained neurological symptoms or overt head injury without an adequate explanation. A clear understanding is required of the pattern of accidental head injury in childhood to inform a decision as to whether non-accidental head injury is possible.

Accidental versus non-accidental head injury

Several studies have compared non-accidental and accidental head injury. Accidental head injuries are most commonly caused by falls in children who are independently mobile. In contrast, non-accidental head injury is seen predominantly in babies under 6 months old who are not yet crawling.

Studies of young children who experienced accidental short falls from less than 1–1.5 metres show that 10–20% sustain an injury that is clinically evident. These injuries are typically to the head and include bumps, bruises, and lacerations. Simple linear skull fractures are sustained in less than 1% of cases. Extradural haemorrhage may be associated with a fracture when the underlying middle meningeal

> Box 6.1 **Features of skull fractures that are associated with serious and fatal non-accidental head injury**
>
> - Fractures that affect more than one bone
> - Depressed fractures
> - Widened fractures
> - Growing fractures
> - Fractures with associated intracranial bleeding

artery is ruptured, but subdural haemorrhages and subarachnoid haemorrhages are rare, and retinal haemorrhages are virtually never seen.

In falls from a height of more than 1.5 metres and falls down stairs or from baby walkers, the incidence of skull fracture rises. These usually are linear, but complex fractures are reported with increasing levels of impact. Subdural and subarachnoid haemorrhages are reported in 1–6% of these cases but retinal haemorrhages are uncommon. The severity of these injuries depends on the height of the fall and the surface texture of impact.

Linear parietal fractures are the commonest skull fractures in both accidental and non-accidental head injury.

Intracranial injuries (subdural haemorrhage, subarachnoid haemorrhage, cerebral injuries), retinal haemorrhages, other extracranial inflicted injuries and an absence of a history of trauma are commonly associated with non-accidental head injury. Road traffic accidents and traumatic head injury can cause severe complex head injuries with associated intracranial and retinal injury similar to those seen in child abuse. These children, however, invariably present with a clear and credible explanation. With the exception of road traffic accidents, the mortality after non-accidental head injury is significantly higher than that from accidental head injuries.

Mechanisms of head injury

The spectrum of clinical features is related to the intensity and type of injury sustained. Impact injuries (direct blows from falls or punches) produce translational forces to the head that may result in swelling, bruising, or lacerations at the site of impact. If the impact is hard enough, the child will sustain a fracture at the point of impact (Box 6.1). Impact is known to cause epidural, subdural, or subarachnoid haemorrhages. There may be coup or contre-coup cerebral injuries.

The term "shaken baby syndrome" implies knowledge of the mechanism of trauma and is best abandoned in favour of non-accidental or inflicted head injury. Perpetrators have admitted to shaking babies, either by holding them around the chest (Fig. 6.2) or by grabbing them by the limbs and swinging them. There is continuing debate in the literature as to whether shaking alone or shaking and impact is necessary to cause non-accidental head injury. The causative mechanism of a subdural haemorrhage is thought to involve acceleration and deceleration forces to the brain with a rotational component, causing rupture of the fine veins that cross the subdural space; these veins then bleed into that space. On the basis of neuropathological findings of localised axonal damage at the craniocervical junction, in the corticospinal tracts, and the cervical cord roots, it has been postulated that some infants who die suffer a stretch injury from cervical hyperflexion-hyperextension (whiplash). **The minimal acceleration–deceleration force required to cause intracerebral injury cannot be defined. However, these types of injury are not recorded in everyday child care and play.**

In a crushing injury, where there is simultaneous pressure on both sides of the skull, symmetrical linear fractures may be produced on either side of the head. Complex linear fractures may result when the tensile forces overcome the elasticity of the skull. The fractures radiate out from the highest points of pressure or impact. This is an uncommon type of injury but has been reported when a baby's

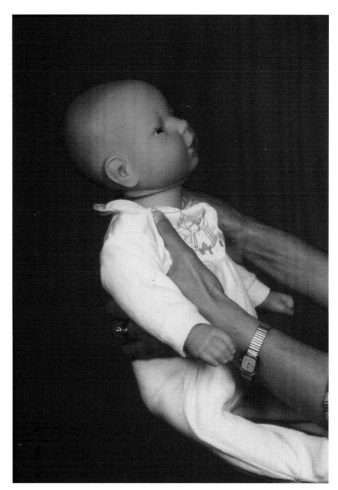

Figure 6.2 Demonstration of shaking with baby model.

head was shut in a car door or when a carer stamped on a child's head in anger.

When a child presents to hospital with a head injury, there are grounds for a child protection investigation if no other cause is apparent, there is no history of trauma, and any history given does not seem to explain the clinical findings (Box 6.2).

Intracranial injury

The incidence of non-accidental head injury with intracranial injury in the UK is estimated to be 21–24 per 100 000 children under 2 years, rising to 35 per 100 000 in infants under 6 months (Fig. 6.3). The associated brain damage results in a high mortality and severe morbidity that includes disability in survivors. Up to 30% of these children die. Deaths are usually the result of uncontrollable brain swelling, and at postmortem examination the most frequent micro-

Box 6.2 **Child protection investigations are advisable if:**

- No other cause is apparent (for example, accident or bleeding diathesis)
- There is no history of trauma
- A history of remote or recent trauma, including that of a short fall, does not seem to explain the clinical findings

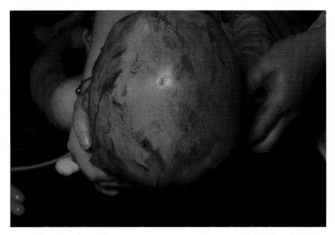

Figure 6.3 Non-accidental, linear lacerations on scalp, caused by a machete.

scopic finding in the brain is global neuronal hypoxia-ischaemia. Brain damage occurs from a cascade of events – ischaemia, hypoxia, and altered vascular permeability – that contributes to further cerebral oedema. Half of survivors sustain complex physical and developmental disabilities. Even those with apparently good recovery may develop learning and behavioural difficulties at school.

Most studies show that about 70% of subdural haemorrhages (SDHs) in infants result from non-accidental head injury, 10% from recognised medical or surgical conditions, and 10% after severe accidental injury such as road traffic accidents; in 10% the cause remains undefined. Subdural haemorrhage in an infant should therefore alert the clinician to the possibility of non-accidental head injury (Box 6.3). About 60–75% of infants with subdural haemorrhage have other manifestations of physical abuse. Therefore, all infants must be evaluated thoroughly to identify the full extent of injury. In the absence of a clear diagnosis of physical abuse, all other causes for the intracranial lesions must be considered and investigated.

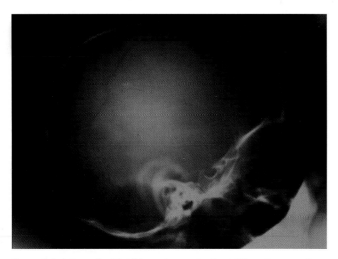

Figure 6.4 A 9 month old child seen by a general practitioner because of a respiratory illness was found to have unexplained bruises over both parietal regions. After referral to the accident and emergency department a lateral skull x ray showed a large fracture crossing the right parietal bone.

Box 6.3 **Assessment of child with subdural haematoma**

Multi-agency team members
- General paediatrician and those with expertise in child protection
- Paediatric neurologist or neurosurgeon, or both
- Neuroradiologist
- Ophthalmologist
- Area child protection team social worker and police

Clinical history
- Full paediatric case history
- Full documentation of all possible explanations for injury

Social and police history
- Identify any previous child protection concerns
- Relevant criminal record of carers

Examination
- Thorough general examination
- Documentation and photographs of injuries
- Monitor head circumference

Laboratory
- Full blood count repeated over first 24–48 hours
- Coagulation screen
- Urea and electrolytes, liver function tests, serum amylase
- Septic screen
- Urine for toxicology and metabolic screen

Ophthalmology
- Examination of both eyes with indirect ophthalmoscopy

Radiology
- Initial cranial computed tomography
- Repeat neuroimaging at 7 and 14 days (MRI scan preferable)
- Discuss neuroimaging with neuroradiologist
- Full skeletal survey according to BPRS guidelines

Clinical management

Children with non-accidental head injury present with various symptoms and signs that vary from subtle and non-specific to dramatic. The history may include poor feeding, vomiting, mild respiratory symptoms, and lethargy (Figs 6.4–6.6); the baby may be drowsy, with seizures, deeply comatose, or dead on arrival. Diagnosis is therefore challenging and requires meticulous assessment and investigation.

The complex nature of abuse demands a multi-agency team approach. The acute paediatric or paediatric neurology team need to work with the child's carers and primary healthcare providers. The clinical skills of the neuroradiologist and ophthalmologist are essential. It is often easier for a paediatrician with expertise in child protection to coordinate the child protection process. Early referral to social services and the police is best practice. The safety of other children in the home must also be considered and a risk assessment done to decide whether the children can remain there. This team approach is also recommended if the child has died before reaching hospital.

History

A thorough history should include details of previous injury, birth

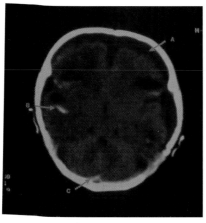 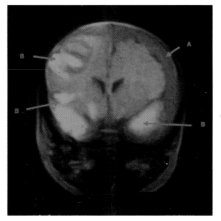 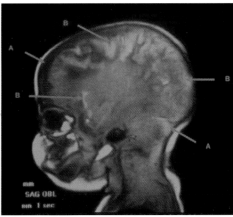

Figure 6.5 A 10-week-old infant presented to the health visitor with irritability and poor feeding and was referred to a paediatrician. He was well cared for and had no signs of external injury. A bulging fontanelle was noted. Left: computed tomogram of brain, axial view, taken on admission to hospital, shows a diffusely abnormal brain with patchy low attenuation areas throughout both cerebral hemispheres. There is a low attenuation subdural effusion anteriorly (A). There are cystic areas within both anterior temporal and frontal lobes that contain high density material, presumably blood (B). The high attenuation area (C) represents a more acute bleed. Middle and right: MRI brain scans were carried out five days later. Coronal view shows bilateral collections of subdural fluid (A). There were high signal areas affecting the right parietal and both temporal regions (B). On the sagittal view, collections of subdural fluid were seen anteriorly and in the posterior fossa (A). High signal areas were seen affecting the gyri in the frontal, posterior parietal, anterior temporal, and occipital regions (B). Appearances indicated an extensive ischaemic haemorrhagic event. The anterior temporal lesions were typical of a shearing injury.

history, and vitamin K status, and full details of explanations of injury (see chapter 2) is also essential. The social and family history are also important because many of these infants may have experienced previous episodes of abuse that were missed during other health visits or possibly during admissions to hospital.

General examination

A careful search must be made for any sign of injury, such as bruises and injuries in the mouth (including the oropharynx) or on the head and scalp and grip marks on the trunk or limbs. There may be a boggy swelling on the scalp, which can be a considerable size. Often, clinical examination reveals no or only minor bruises to the scalp, but haematomas may be seen at postmortem examination on reflection of the scalp. There may be other skin injuries including burns, scalds, and bite marks. The examination must include an inspection of the anogenital region. All injuries must be carefully documented. Photographs are helpful, where available.

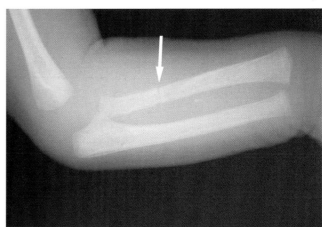

(b)

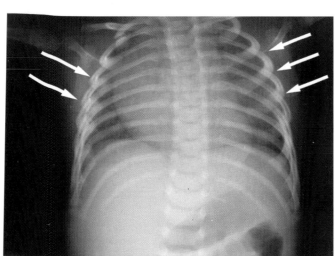

(a)

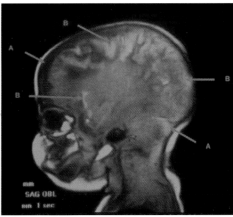

(c)

Figure 6.6 A 6 week old baby presented to hospital with irritability. Bilateral small subdural haemorrhages were seen on an MRI scan. Skeletal survey showed multiple bilateral rib fractures (a), a transverse fracture of the radius (b), and a metaphyseal fracture of the distal femur (c).

Table 6.1 Differential diagnoses of subdural haemorrhage in an infant

Cause of SDH	Comment
Trauma	
Non-accidental head injury	Commonest cause; often associated with other inflicted injuries and retinal haemorrhages
Accidental head injury	May occur in high falls; whiplash injury in major trauma – for example, road traffic accident Minor household falls rarely cause subdural haemorrhage Retinal haemorrhages associated only with severe injury
Neurosurgical complications	Commonly reported as a postoperative complication of neurosurgery
Perinatal	
Fetal	Infrequently reported on fetal ultrasound scans
Labour	May occur after childbirth, most commonly after instrumental delivery. Resolves after four weeks, as do most associated retinal haemorrhages
Cranial malformations	
Aneurysms; arachnoid cysts	Spontaneous bleeding from vascular malformations, when present; less serious trauma can result in a bleed. Both unlikely to be associated with retinal haemorrhages unless intracranial pressure is raised
Cranial infections	
Meningitis	Postinfective subdural effusions may be associated with retinal haemorrhages if there has been severe vasculitis
Coagulation or haematological disorders	
Leukaemia; sickle cell anaemia; disseminated intravascular coagulation; haemophilia; von Willebrand's disease; haemorrhagic disease of the newborn; platelet or coagulation factor disorders	Diagnosis by coagulation and other haematological investigations. All may be associated with retinal haemorrhages
Metabolic or biochemical disorders	
Glutaric aciduria	Associated with widening of subdural space, with stretching and rupture of subdural vessels, causing subdural haemorrhage
Hypernatraemia	Subdural haemorrhage described in association with salt poisoning, hypernatraemic dehydration. Hypernatraemia may also be a complication of the intracranial trauma

Laboratory investigations

Most of these infants present acutely ill, and investigations should be performed as for any ill infant. Full blood count may reveal rapidly falling haemoglobin concentrations that reflect the extreme clinical state of the patient or indicate blood loss elsewhere (for example, abdomen, subaponeurotic bleed). Coagulation studies and septic screen will exclude major bleeding disorders or infection. Liver function tests, serum amylase activity, urea and electrolyte concentrations, and abdominal ultrasonography may be useful if intra-abdominal injury is suspected. Urine should be sent for toxicology and metabolic screen.

Ophthalmology

When physical abuse is suspected, an ophthalmologist should carry out an indirect ophthalmoscopic examination as soon as possible. Retinal haemorrhages are present in about 80% of infants with subdural haemorrhage from non-accidental head injury (see chapter 7).

Neuroimaging

Neuroimaging should be performed in any infant in whom non-accidental head injury is suspected and in those who present with unexplained neurological symptoms, retinal haemorrhage, unexplained fractures, or injuries to the head or in whom a lumbar puncture (performed to exclude meningitis in a sick infant) shows uniformly blood stained cerebrospinal fluid. Computed tomography is the most widely available neuroimaging technique. It is a good method for detecting an acute subdural bleed and differentiating between subarachnoid and subdural blood.

Magnetic resonance imaging (MRI) is used as first line investigation where it is readily available and paediatric neuroradiologists are available to interpret findings. Computed tomography or magnetic resonance imaging should be repeated a few days later. Magnetic resonance imaging is a more sensitive method for identifying smaller bleeds, especially in those areas less well seen on computed tomography. It is especially useful for those with cerebral oedema and ischaemic changes, which are well demonstrated by diffusion weighted magnetic resonance imaging. In all cases a neuroradiologist with paediatric expertise should review the results because each year an average district general hospital will have only one or two cases of head injury related to child abuse.

Typical findings on neuroimaging are of small and multiple bleeds, often of different density. The haemorrhages occur most commonly over the cerebral convexity and are seen in the interhemispheric fissure and middle and posterior fossae. Associated injuries may include subarachnoid haemorrhage, small intracerebral bleeds or tears, and focal or generalised cerebral oedema. The latter arises from associated hypoxic or ischaemic damage and is associated with a generally poor prognosis.

Skeletal radiology

It is essential to perform a skeletal survey to exclude associated fractures that are found in up to 50% of diagnosed cases of non-accidental head injury. The commonest fractures involve the ribs, followed by skull and long bones, and metaphyseal fractures. Vertebral fractures have also been reported and highlight the importance of thorough investigation to exclude injury to the skeleton or spinal cord. Other radiological studies will be dictated by clinical need.

Differential diagnoses

When a subdural haemorrhage is associated with inflicted injuries there is a high probability of non-accidental head injury. Table 6.1 lists other causes of subdural haemorrhage, most of which have distinguishing clinical features. The infant with an isolated subdural haemorrhage and no additional risk factors of physical abuse presents the greatest diagnostic challenge. The clinician has little evidence to support a diagnosis of probable non-accidental head injury and yet may be unable to exclude the possibility. It is important in these cases to ensure that all diagnostic alternatives have been fully explored and a multi-agency risk assessment completed. Consultation with clinical specialists is recommended and thorough investigations to exclude the more rare causes.

Further reading

Datta S, Stoodley N, Jayawant J, Renowden S, Kemp A. Neuroradiological aspects of subdural haemorrhages. *Arch Dis Child* 2005;90:947–51.

(Editorial) Shaken baby syndrome. *Arch Dis Child* 2006;91:205–6.

Hobbs C, Childs AM, Wynne J, Livingston J, Seal A. Subdural haematoma and effusion in infancy: an epidemiological study. Arch Dis Child 2005;90:952–5.

Jayawant S, Rawlinson A, Gibbon F, Price J, Schulte J, Sharples P, et al. Subdural haemorrhages in infants: population based study. *BMJ* 1998;317:1558–61.

Kemp AM, Stoodley N, Cobley C, Coles L, Kemp KW. Apnoea and brain swelling in non-accidental head injury. *Arch Dis Child* 2003;88:472–6.

Kemp AM. Investigating subdural haemorrhage in infants. *Arch Dis Child* 2002;86:98–102.

Lyons TJ, Oates K, Falling out of bed: a relatively benign occurrence. *Pediatrics* 1993;92:125–7.

Reece RM, Sege R, Childhood head injuries – accidental or inflicted? *Arch Pediatr Adolesc Med* 2000;154:11–5.

Stoodley N. Neuroimaging in non-accidental head injury: if, when, why and how. *Clin Radiol* 2005;60:22–30.

Towner D, Castro MA, Eby-Wilkens E, Gilbert WM. Effect of mode of delivery in nulliparous woman on neonatal intracranial injury. *N Engl J Med* 1999;341:1709–14.

Whitby EH, Griffiths PD, Rutter S. Frequency and natural history of subdural haemorrhages in babies and relation to obstetric factors. *Lancet* 2004;363:846–51.

CHAPTER 7

Ophthalmic Presentations

Alex V Levin

Virtually any ocular injury may be the result of child abuse. Ocular injury is the presenting sign of physical abuse in 4–6% of cases of child abuse. There are several ocular abnormalities that, when found, suggest trauma has occurred, even when no history of trauma is given (Table 7.1). Non-compliance with medical treatment and neglect can also result in permanent loss of vision. Sexual abuse may be the route of transmission of a sexually transmitted disease to the eyes. Abused children also may develop functional symptoms such as blinking, unusual visual phenomena, or non-organic loss of vision.

Detection of ocular manifestations

A complete eye examination, including dilatation of the pupil for retinal examination by an ophthalmologist, is usually indicated whenever physical abuse is suspected in a child under 4 years old. Examination with only a direct ophthalmoscope should not replace complete retinal examination by an ophthalmologist, which can be

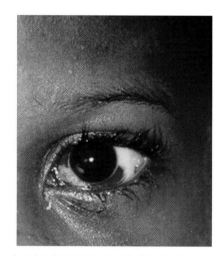

Figure 7.1 Left periocular ecchymosis and subconjunctival haemorrhage in child who had been beaten with a belt. Although the target was not the child's eye, the belt "unintentionally" caused the injuries together with hyphema and bruising of the retina (commotio retinae).

Table 7.1 Ocular signs that could indicate trauma

		Comment
Eyelids	Laceration*, ecchymosis	Unilateral/bilateral ecchymosis may follow forehead trauma
Eyeball	Ruptured globe* (corneal/ scleral laceration)	
Conjunctiva	Subconjunctival haemorrhage	Also from suffocation/ strangulation
Cornea	Chemical burns, scars	Especially when acquired bilaterally
Anterior chamber	Hyphema	
Lens	Cataract; dislocated lens	Especially when acquired unilaterally
Vitreous	Haemorrhage; detached vitreous base*	
Retina	Haemorrhage, contusion* (Berlin's oedema, commotio retinae (Fig. 7.1)); detached retina	

*Pathognomonic for trauma.

accomplished only with the indirect (head mounted) ophthalmoscope. Indirect ophthalmoscopy may show changes, particularly in the peripheral retina, that cannot be viewed with the direct ophthalmoscope. These findings, including peripheral haemorrhages, may have particular importance in identifying an abused child. Use of the direct ophthalmoscope by the primary care or emergency doctor, however, can be a useful screening test. The pupils should be dilated with one drop of phenylephrine 2.5% and cyclopentolate 1% (except in premature infants being examined before their due date or infants who were small for gestational age, in whom cyclopentolate 0.5% is preferred). If there is concern about using pupillary reactivity to monitor a child's neurological status, the cyclopentolate (duration of mydriasis up to one day) may be omitted or one eye can be dilated at a time. With phenylephrine alone, pupillary reactivity should return in four to six hours.

Despite the value of a positive direct ophthalmoscope examination, the absence of abnormalities, in particular retinal haemorrhages, does not obviate the need for consultation with an ophthalmologist (Box 7.1). This is particularly true when injuries from shaking are suspected. If an ophthalmologist is readily available it is best to forego pupillary dilatation unless it is specifically requested, as the ophthalmologist may wish to examine the child before pupillary dilatation.

When a child less than 4 years old dies suddenly for no apparent reason, gross and histological examination of the eyeballs and orbital tissue, including the optic nerve, should be included as part of the postmortem examination. Both eyeballs should be removed, preferably with the entire orbital contents, from a combined anterior and intracranial approach after removal of the brain. After formalin fixation (recommended 72 hours) these tissues should be sectioned *en bloc*. Any gross or histological abnormalities should be photographed. If the pathologist is unable to remove the orbital tissues with the eyeball, then the entire globe, along with a long segment of optic nerve, should be removed from an anterior approach. Removal of the globe with or without the orbital contents does not cause a cosmetically apparent deformity should the body be on view at the funeral.

Retinal haemorrhages

Retinal haemorrhages are one of the fundamental signs in victims of abusive repeated acceleration–deceleration trauma (e.g. shaking),

occurring in about 80% of cases. These haemorrhages may occur in front of (preretinal), within (intraretinal), or under (subretinal) the retina (Figs 7.2–7.4). They are usually bilateral, but unilateral or asymmetric distribution is well recognised. Traumatic retinoschisis is a form of retinal injury, usually with haemorrhage, that has been reported only in shaken babies. Because of concomitant shaking of the vitreous gel, which is adherent to the posterior retina in young infants, the retinal layers are split apart to cause a dome shaped cavity, which may be partially or completely filled with blood. Some observers have incorrectly described similar retinal abnormalities as subhyaloid haemorrhage – a collection of blood between the retina and vitreous gel. Schisis can be distinguished from subhyaloid blood by the presence of a white or haemorrhagic circumlinear outline to the lesion with or without an associated retinal fold or ridge and retinal blood vessels that may be elevated on the surface of the schisis. A similar (but not identical) ridge has been reported in two cases of severe crush injury. Other studies of crush injury have not shown this finding.

Smaller "cystic" cavities containing blood can be seen elsewhere in the retina, especially overlying blood vessels. When found over blood vessels these cavities do not seem to have as much diagnostic specificity. Although macular retinoschisis lesions may heal with little effect on vision, circular folds and circumlinear scars within the retina may serve as a marker of previous abuse.

Other effects of shaking include retinal detachment and atrophy of the optic nerve. The latter seems to be due to shaking injury involving the orbital contents behind the globe. The intracranial approach to removal of the entire orbital contents, as described above, is designed to identify such injury.

The exact mechanism by which retinal haemorrhages occur in the shaken infant is becoming clearer. Increased intracranial pressure,

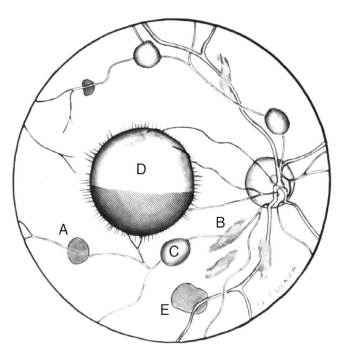

Figure 7.2 A: intraretinal blot haemorrhage, blood vessel passes into and through haemorrhage; B: superficial intraretinal flame-shaped haemorrhage; C: preretinal haemorrhage, blood vessel obscured; D: traumatic retinoschisis; E: subretinal haemorrhage, vessel runs over haemorrhage. Reproduced from Ludwig S, Kornberg AE. *Child abuse. A medical reference.* New York: Churchill Livingstone, 1991.

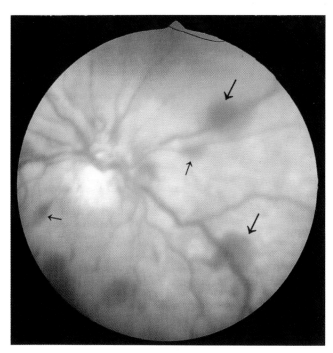

Figure 7.3 Retinal haemorrhages in an abused child. Small arrows indicate flame-shaped haemorrhages. Large arrows indicate "blot" intraretinal haemorrhages. No traumatic retinoschisis was seen in this child.

subdural or subarachnoid haemorrhage (Terson syndrome), and chest compression by the perpetrator's hand or cardiopulmonary resuscitation have been shown to play little, if any, relevant role. Several studies – retrospective, prospective, and multicentre – and animal models have concluded that retinal haemorrhages rarely, if ever, occur after cardiopulmonary resuscitation and involve only a small number of intraretinal or preretinal haemorrhages around the optic nerve. Retinopathy from chest compression (Purtscher retinopathy), which is characterised by white intraretinal patches, has not been observed, to my knowledge, after cardiopulmonary resuscitation. Direct shaking injury to the retina due to retinal-vitreous traction/shearing seems to be the most important factor in causing shaking related retinal haemorrhage.

In the differential diagnosis of retinal haemorrhage in infants and young toddlers, the key findings are the number of haemorrhages, the pattern of distribution, and the types of haemorrhage. Retinal haemorrhage in children <4 years old is rarely caused by accidental head trauma and is particularly rare after short falls. When a moderate number of retinal haemorrhages are present the history of the incident is usually of such a severe event as to be obvious and sufficient to exclude the possibility of child abuse. Even with major trauma such as road traffic accidents, these haemorrhages usually are few in number, confined to the posterior aspect of the retina (posterior pole), and exclusively intraretinal and preretinal. In extremely severe life threatening events, such as a pedestrian struck by a vehicle, more severe haemorrhage might be seen. This is different from the retinal haemorrhages of the shaken baby, which in two thirds of cases are too numerous to count, distributed diffusely throughout the retina with extension beyond the posterior pole to the retinal edge (ora serrata), and found at all layers including subretinal, and, in one third, include macular traumatic retinoschisis.

> **Normal activities of childhood such as throwing a baby into the air and catching, jogging with a baby in a backpack, or bouncing a baby on one's knee do not cause retinal haemorrhage.**

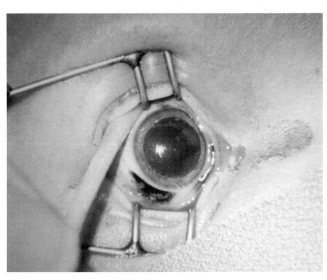

Figure 7.4 Subconjunctival haemorrhage in an infant who died as a result of non-accidental suffocation by the parent (cotton swab is being used to hold the eye in position).

Other systemic conditions can cause retinal haemorrhages in young children. Usually they are identified easily by a full history and physical examination with appropriate laboratory investigations where indicated and an examination by an ophthalmologist familiar with paediatric eye disease. They include severe hypertension, fulminant meningitis, vasculitis, sepsis, endocarditis, coagulopathy, leukaemia, cyanotic congenital heart disease, vitamin K deficiency, and malaria. Retinal haemorrhages are commonly seen after a normal delivery. The incidence is highest after ventouse (vacuum) delivery, followed by spontaneous vaginal delivery, forceps assisted delivery, and, least, caesarean section. Flame haemorrhages resolve within two weeks of birth. Intraretinal haemorrhages usually resolve within four weeks but can, rarely, persist for up to six weeks. Seizures rarely, if ever, cause retinal haemorrhage; in the only reported case, a small number of flame haemorrhages around the optic nerve were present in one eye of a patient who was not evaluated thoroughly for other possible causes. Diabetes mellitus, childhood vaccinations, and haemoglobinopathies such as sickle cell anaemia do not cause retinal haemorrhages in the age group most likely to incur severe shaking.

Sexually transmitted diseases

The exact diagnostic relevance of sexually transmitted diseases affecting the eye in non-neonatal prepubertal children remains somewhat unclear (Table 7.2). Two retrospective studies have identified cases in which gonorrhoeal conjunctivitis was apparently transmitted non-sexually. Gonorrhoea cannot be transmitted to genital or oropharyngeal locations by any route other than sexual contact. Perhaps the mucosal lining of the eye represents a special site receptive to non-sexual transmission. In each of the cases of non-sexual transmission there was a family member who had a genital infection, and all investigations for sexual abuse in the child yielded negative

Table 7.2 Ocular manifestations of sexually transmitted disease

Gonorrhoea*	Purulent conjunctivitis with possible spontaneous corneal perforation
Chlamydia†	Chronic conjunctivitis
Herpes simplex virus*	Keratitis, conjunctivitis, intraocular inflammation, retinal necrosis
Human papilloma virus†	Conjunctival papillomas
HIV*	Intraocular inflammation, opportunistic retinal infections (for example, cytomegalovirus, toxoplasmosis), optic neuropathy, eye movement disorders
Syphilis	Intraocular inflammation, retinal vasculitis, optic neuropathy, eye movement disorders, and many other ocular abnormalities
Pubic lice†	Eyelash infestation
Molluscum*	Eyelid/periorbital lesions with possible secondary conjunctivitis

*Possible non-sexual transmission to eye in non-neonates has been documented.
†Route of transmission to eye not well studied. Late symptoms after neonatal non-sexual transmission may occur.

results (including negative cultures for other sexually transmitted diseases at other sites and an interview with the child by a person skilled and experienced in child sexual abuse cases).

Syphilis is the only organism that results in ocular effects exclusively through sexual contact. Although the presence of any other sexually transmitted disease should, at the very least, prompt consideration that possible covert sexual abuse has occurred, non-sexual transmission remains a theoretical possibility. With each of the infections, perhaps excepting ocular herpes and molluscum, a complete evaluation for sexual abuse is indicated. Reporting to child protection agencies should be reserved for those cases in which further evaluation confirms the suspicion of sexual abuse or fails to offer another plausible explanation.

Chronic and unusual visual symptoms or signs

Children may present with one of many functional ocular symptoms, including blinking, photophobia, eyelid pulling, eye rolling, and visual disturbances. Covert abuse is a rare cause of such symptoms but must always be considered when stress factors that are commonly associated with functional illness are investigated. Likewise, chronic medically unexplainable ocular signs or symptoms such as recurrent conjunctivitis or abnormalities in pupillary size

should provoke consideration of Munchausen syndrome by proxy (fabricated and induced illness) in the appropriate clinical setting (see page 67). In addition, recurrent periorbital cellulitis has been reported as a manifestation of fabricated or induced illness. Nystagmus, abnormalities of the pupil, or strabismus may result from covert poisoning.

Further reading

Adams G, Ainsworth J, Butler L, Bonshek R, Clarke M, Doran R, et al. Ophthalmology Child Abuse Working Party, Royal College of Ophthalmologists. Update from the ophthalmology child abuse working party-Royal College of Ophthalmologists. *Eye* 2004;18:795–8.

Kivlin JD, Simons KB, Lazoritz S, Ruttum MS: Shaken baby syndrome. *Ophthalmology* 2000;107:1246–54.

Levin AV. Retinal haemorrhages and child abuse. In: David TJ, ed. *Recent advances in paediatrics. No 18*. London: Churchill Livingstone, 2000:151–219.

Levin AV, Wygnanski-Jaffe T, Shafiq A, Smith C, Enzenauer RW, Elder J, et al. Postmortem orbital findings in shaken baby syndrome. *Am J Ophthalmol* 2006;142:233–40.

Morad Y, Kim YM, Armstrong DC, Huyer D, Mian M, Levin AV. Correlation between retinal abnormalities and intracranial abnormalities in the shaken baby syndrome. *Am J Ophthalmol* 2002;134:354–9.

Taylor D, Ophthalmology Child Abuse Working Party. Child abuse and the eye. *Eye* 1999;13:2–10.

CHAPTER 8

Visceral Injury

Russell Migita, Kenneth Feldman

Epidemiology

Visceral trauma is an infrequent result of child abuse, serious cases being associated with only 5% of physically abused children. It is, however, one of the most lethal forms of child abuse, with a mortality near 50%. Abdominal injury is second only to head trauma as a cause of fatal paediatric physical abuse. Visceral injuries due to child abuse are under-recognised and under-reported.

Most deaths result from haemorrhage, solid organ injury, or peritonitis after hollow viscus perforation. As in accidental trauma, 90% of thoracoabdominal physical abuse is caused by blunt injury. Whereas the peak incidence of non-accidental head trauma is during infancy and the peak incidence of accidental trauma is during the early school years, the peak of non-accidental thoracoabdominal injury is during the toddler years. This may be partly because of the tendency for negative behaviour in toddlers and problems over toilet training. Of the children who present with severe visceral trauma, 20% will have coexisting, major extra-abdominal injury such as injuries to extremities or the head (Tables 8.1 and 8.2).

Life threatening thoracic injuries are much less common than abdominal injuries. Most chest injuries do not have associated bruising, and intrathoracic injuries, other than rib fractures, are rare. Although inflicted abdominal injury similarly is unlikely to cause signs of trauma that are visible on inspection, none the less there

Table 8.1 Frequency of mortality and serious injury associated with accidental versus abdominal trauma in two US series of cases of paediatric abdominal trauma

	Accident	Abuse (Seattle)	Abuse (Philadelphia)
Number	139	17	22
Mortality	29 (21%)	9 (53%)	10 (45%)
Abdominal haemorrhage	2 (7%)	4 (44%)	9 (90%)
Abdominal sepsis	NA	4 (44%)	1 (10%)
Head injury	19 (66%)	1 (12%)	NA
Fatal hollow viscus perforation	2/7 (28%)	5/7 (71%)	1/5 (20%)

NA=Not available

Table 8.2 Comparison of characteristics of accidental versus abusive injury in the same series

	Accident	Abuse (Seattle)	Abuse (Philadelphia)
Number	139	17	22
Mean age (years)	7.5	2.5	2
Extra-abdominal injury	NA	65%	100%
Major extra-abdominal injury	NA	18%	NA
Delay in care	9% >3 hours	100% >3 hours	Mean 13 hours
Abdominal bruise	NA	2	NA

NA=Not available

may be severe internal damage. Difficulty with visual diagnosis, the young age of the children involved, and delayed presentation may all be factors contributing to the high morbidity and mortality associated with abusive visceral injury.

Presentation

Often there is little historical information to suggest abuse. Carers usually fail to mention, or frankly deny, trauma. Doctors must always keep the possibility of abuse in mind. As in other cases of child abuse, it is important to consider the developmental abilities of the child and whether the stated mechanism of injury was likely to have caused the observed injury. Inflicted visceral injuries are more likely than accidental injuries to present more than 12 hours after the event. In most cases of accidental injury children are brought directly from the scene of the incident.

Diagnosis of blunt abdominal trauma is particularly difficult (Fig. 8.1). Abdominal wall bruising is an inconsistent finding, being reported in 12%, 29% and 75% of victim series, and leads to delay in presentation and diagnosis. Hollow visceral injuries often present with vague gastrointestinal complaints. Solid visceral injuries may present with lethargy or coma, secondary to evolving haemorrhagic shock. Gut necrosis or perforation can cause peritonitis. Traumatic pancreatitis often presents with vomiting and may come to attention weeks later due to an obstructive pseudocyst. Presenting signs and symptoms of visceral injury may include bilious or non-bilious

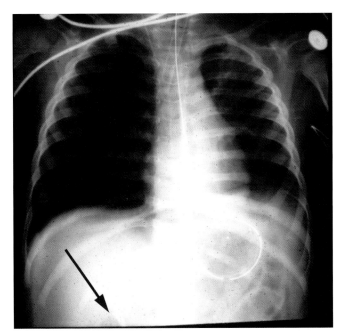

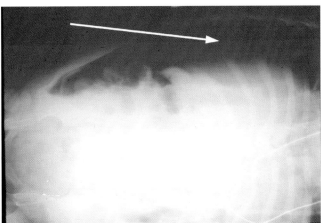

Figure 8.1 This 2 year old presented in shock with a distended abdomen. The carer claimed that a 3 year old sibling had been hitting him. Air surrounds the falciform ligament, indicating an intestinal perforation. Below: lateral decubitus abdomen radiograph of the same boy. Arrow denotes free air. At autopsy, he was found to have a peripancreatic haemorrhage and pus in the abdomen.

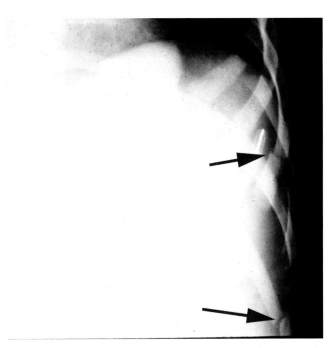

Figure 8.2 Rib fractures in a 5 year old who died from a torn omentum and haemorrhagic shock. Father later admitted karate chopping the child across epigastrium.

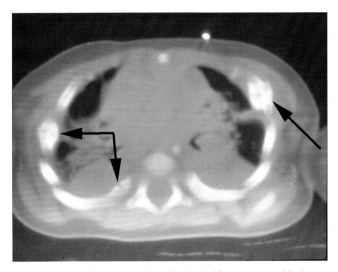

Figure 8.3 This child ultimately died of a subdural haematoma and brain injury. Computed tomogram shows three rib fractures at various stages of healing. Note location of fractures. With compression of the chest by an adult, the posterior portions of the ribs articulate posteriorly and are fractured by impingement against the transverse process of the vertebra.

vomiting, abdominal pain, alteration in level of consciousness, reduced activity, haemodynamic instability, and fever.

Distinguishing those with potentially serious intra-abdominal injury is difficult. A careful search should be made for extra-abdominal injury, such as unexplained bruising or tenderness.

Mode of injury

Children are more prone than adults to intra-abdominal injury from blunt trauma. Their abdominal walls are thinner, with less interposed fat and muscle to protect the viscera. They also have more flexible ribs that cover proportionally less of the abdomen. Children have organs that are proportionally larger, predisposing them to multiple organ injury. Finally, gastric or bowel distension due to

crying or food intake may lead to a higher likelihood of rupture after impact.

Thoracic injury is most often confined to the chest wall; the most common reported injury is rib fractures (Figs 8.2 and 8.3). Any part of the rib can be injured, but injury to the posterolateral aspects of an infant's or toddler's ribs, without a history of major trauma, strongly suggests abuse. Chest compressions during cardiopulmonary resuscitation (CPR) are often claimed to be the cause of rib fractures in infants and toddlers. These fractures, however, are usually old at the time of the cardiopulmonary resuscitation and the cause of the collapse is not explained (see chapter 5).

Intrathoracic injury is rare because children have a very compliant, but protective, chest wall. High energy blows can cause pneumothorax, haemothorax, or chylothorax (Figs 8.4 and 8.5) as a result of lacerations of lung parenchyma or intercostal blood or lymph vessels. Blows can cause focal pulmonary or cardiac contusions. Inflicted airway or major vascular injury is rare. Pharyngeal, oesophageal, or tracheal injury, mediastinal air, or infection, however, can result from foreign objects inserted from the mouth. Commotio cordis is a rare cause of terminal arrhythmia after a direct direct blow to the sternum.

Inflicted solid organ injury most often occurs after a blow to the ribs or upper abdomen. Solid organs of children have a weak internal structure and can be damaged by direct impact or by crushing of the abdominal viscera against the vertebral column. In accidental trauma, this usually results from whole body inertial events such as being hit by a vehicle in the street. Although injury to the spleen is the most common accidental abdominal injury, it is infrequent with abuse, probably because the rib cage protects the spleen from direct blows. In abuse, hollow visceral injuries usually result from a punch or kick to the hypogastric area. This may result in organ rupture with resultant peritonitis. Contused bowel may later develop haematomas, which can lead to either obstruction or necrosis. Duodenal haematomas generally present with bilious vomiting. Necrosis of the bowel can result in delayed perforation and peritonitis. Because of delayed presentation to care, these injuries are associated with shock and sepsis and may be fatal. Strictures may develop several days to weeks after a contusing injury to the intestines, and the child may present with vomiting or distension. Comparable accidental injuries to the intestine can occur from falls on to bicycle

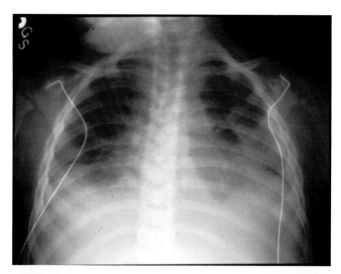

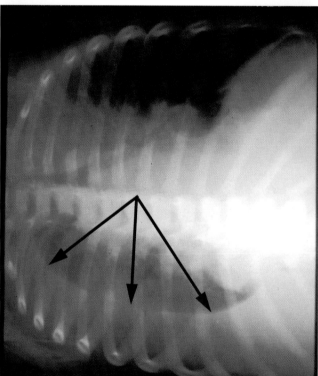

Figure 8.5 Chylothorax (top: upright anteroposterior view; bottom: right lateral decubitus view). This child aged 15 months had x ray investigation because of respiratory distress and was found to have several anterior lumbar vertebral body avulsion fractures, as well as a right parietal and left tibial fracture. The chylous fluid level is seen when the child is placed on the right side. Chylothorax is much less common than haemothorax and can be caused by compressive forces on the chest wall.

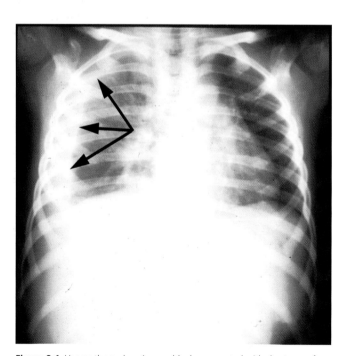

Figure 8.4 Haemothorax in a 4 year old who presented with shortness of breath and multiple bruises. Several acute rib fractures were noted after the haemothorax was drained.

handlebars and injuries caused by vehicle lap belts. Shearing of the intestine or damage to its vascular supply, leading to mesenteric or cavomesenteric disruption, can occur after rapid body deceleration or focal blows at sites of bowel fixation. The duodenojejunal junction at the ligament of Treitz (Fig. 8.6) is the area most prone to this type of injury.

In rapid deceleration, such as when the child is thrown against the ground, the free jejunal section can shear away from the fixed

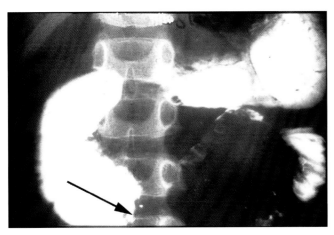

Figure 8.6 The first and second segments of the duodenum appear normal, but only small amounts of contrast pass through the ligament of Treitz. The child presented with bilious vomiting and had a duodenal haematoma leading to intestinal obstruction.

duodenum. As with chest compressions and thoracic injury, cardiopulmonary resuscitation and the Heimlich manoeuvre have been claimed as the cause of serious abdominal injury. Such children, however, usually have evidence of internal injuries that precede any intervention by a rescuer. There are isolated case reports of liver injury due to cardiopulmonary resuscitation or a Heimlich manoeuvre applied over the lower rib margin, which seem reliable. These may be because the lower position of the child's liver makes it susceptible to shearing force from the rib margin.

Diagnosis

Diagnosis can be challenging, especially shortly after injury. There is little empirical data characterising the sequence of signs and symptoms after these injuries. However, we can assume that abusive events cause immediate abdominal pain. Most children have ongo-

ing symptoms, although they may be subtle enough for clinicians to miss the diagnosis. Worsening symptoms due to evolving haemorrhagic shock, peritonitis, or delayed rupture of devitalised bowel eventually become too severe for carers to ignore. At that stage they commonly say that the child had been well but suddenly became ill. Such a history is incompatible with evolving haemorrhagic shock, peritonitis, and other deteriorating intra-abdominal conditions. The obviously critically injured child should be managed according to standard trauma protocols, with initial evaluation and stabilisation of airway, breathing, and circulation.

In general, most abused children can be evaluated with physical examination and urinalysis alone. Routine laboratory tests for a child with findings suggesting abdominal trauma may include a complete blood count with reticulocyte count, prothrombin time/partial thromboplastin time (PT/PTT); blood serum aspartate aminotransferase (AST)/serum alanine aminotransferase (ALT), amylase/lipase activity, urea, electrolytes, and creatinine concentration; and urinalysis. Usually plain abdominal films yield normal results, unless considerable amounts of free air or fluid are present (Figs 8.7 and 8.8). Upright or decubitus films are more likely to show small amounts of free air. Children with raised hepatocellular or pancreatic enzyme activity, who do not require emergency surgery, should have abdominal imaging with computed tomography or ultrasonography. Cranial computed tomography is also indicated in infants less than 6 months with evidence of physical abuse or in any abused child with altered consciousness.

If the timing of the injury is in question, serial transaminase activities, packed cell volume, and reticulocyte count may be useful. The AST will generally rise and fall before the ALT. Immediately after injury, the packed cell volume and reticulocyte count should be normal. By several hours after injury, haemodilution may cause a drop in the packed cell volume. Polychromasia and a reticulocyte response develop in about two days. If there is an indication of severe injury to the abdominal wall or other muscle injury, urine screening for myoglobin, serum creatinine kinase, and aldolase should be done.

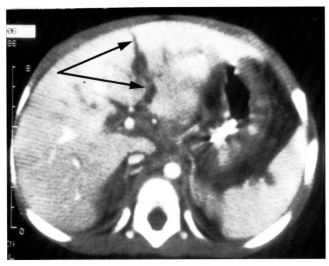

Figure 8.7 This 1 year old presented with tachypnoea, lethargy, distended abdomen, and multiple bruises. Note liver laceration secondary to epigastric blow.

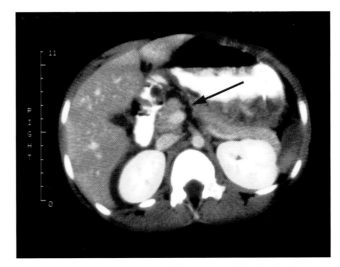

Figure 8.8 This child aged 7 was struck by a 14 year old sibling in the epigastric region of the abdomen. On presentation to the hospital, the child was vomiting and had decompensated shock. Arrows indicate an area of pancreatic transection.

These problems require extra fluids to be given for renal protection and monitoring of renal function.

Electrocardiography or echocardiography may be indicated if cardiac injury is suspected. Acute rib fractures can be difficult to recognise on plain radiographs and may be easier to see with oblique views. If early identification is important, scintigraphy is indicated. Otherwise, follow-up films in 10–14 days to look for healing are appropriate. Computed tomograms of the chest and neck are useful to identify pharyngeal, oesophageal, tracheal, and lung injuries. Endoscopy or contrast radiographs may be needed.

A continuing collaboration between paediatric, surgical, and pathology teams is important to establish the timing of injury, especially for hollow viscus injury with delayed presentation. Often the surgeon has the initial suspicion that the injury might be inflicted. The extent of intra-abdominal inflammation, the vital reaction at the injury site, and whether perforations are primary or secondary to necrosis of the bowel wall help in determining timing.

Treatment

Treatment regimens for acute intrathoracic and abdominal trauma are complicated. Briefly, attention should be paid first to securing the patient's airway and breathing. Intravenous access should be established as necessary and shock should be treated with isotonic saline, blood products, or vasoactive medications. Surgical exploration is required in children with evidence of peritonitis or perforation. Evidence of ongoing blood loss, resulting in cardiovascular instability, despite fluid support, warrants surgical exploration. Most children with blunt abdominal trauma may be managed expectantly with symptomatic support. Adjunctive antibiotics are indicated for peritonitis or perforation.

Further reading

Barnes PM, Norton CM, Dunstan FD, Kemp AM, Sibert JR. Abdominal injury due to child abuse. *Lancet* 2005;366:234–35.

Cooper A, Floyd T, Barlow B, Niemirska M, Ludwig S, Seidl T, et al. Major blunt abdominal trauma due to child abuse. *J Trauma* 1988;28:1483–7.

Cooper A. Thoracoabdominal trauma. In: Ludwig S, Kornberg AE, eds. *Child abuse: a medical reference.* 2nd ed. New York: Churchill Livingstone, 1992:131–50.

Ledbetter DJ, Hatch EI, Feldman KW, Fligner CL, Tapper D. Diagnostic and surgical implications of child abuse. *Arch Surg* 1988;128:1101–5.

Ng CS, Hall CM, Shaw DG. The range of visceral manifestations of non-accidental injury. *Arch Dis Child* 1997;77:167–74.

Roaten JB, Patrick DA, Bensard DD, Hendrickson RJ, Ventrees T, Sirotnak AP, et al. Visceral injuries in nonaccidental trauma: spectrum of injury and outcomes. *Am J Surg* 2005;190:827–9.

Wood J, Rubin DM, Nance ML, Christian CW. Distinguishing inflicted versus accidental abdominal injuries in young children. *J Trauma* 2005;59:1203–8.

CHAPTER 9

Poisoning

Roy Meadow

Toxbase, an online database, is the primary source of information in the United Kingdom:
www.spib.axl.co.uk
For complex cases, specialist advice is available by telephone:
Tel: 0870 600 6266
The centre directs callers to local poison information centres, which throughout the day and night provide advice on most aspects of poisoning. Some also advise on laboratory analytical services

Accidental poisoning is common; non-accidental (deliberate) poisoning is uncommon but more serious (Table 9.1). Accidental poisoning usually occurs in toddlers aged 2 to 4, who explore the world with their mouth and try out any medicines, tablets, or household products that they find. Such events usually occur at home in the daytime with the carer nearby. The parent finds the child with an empty bottle in the bathroom or kitchen and is unsure how much the child has ingested; help is sought promptly. Usually the child has swallowed little or nothing, and it is a poisoning scare rather than a true poisoning event.

Table 9.1 Characteristics of poisoning

	Accidental	Non-accidental
Age	1.5–4 years (rare in those aged <1 or >5)	Any age
Presentation	Poisoning scare or emergency	Unusual symptoms or illnesses
Substance	Drugs; household or gardening product; berries	Usually a prescribed drug
No of substances ingested	One	Sometimes more than one
Amount ingested	Usually none or little	Considerable
Symptoms	Uncommon	Common
Severe illness or death	Very rare	Less rare
Preceding unusual illness (factitious)	Absent	Common
No of episodes	One; recurrence rare	Recurrence common

Breastfed infants are occasionally affected by drugs in their mother's milk. Young children may be affected by their parents' recreational drug use by passive inhalation or active administration. Deliberate self overdose occurs with increasing incidence after the age of 10; its identification is usually obvious. Nevertheless, in all these cases, evidence of other forms of abuse or of unexpected deaths in siblings should be sought, and the child protection register checked. Repeated presentations for accidental poisoning should lead to consideration of possible neglect and inadequate safety and supervision at home.

Less than 15% of the thousands of children who present to hospital because of accidental poisoning develop symptoms from the substance; death is extremely rare. Death from non-accidental poisoning is more common.

The commonest substances used to poison children are drugs that have been prescribed for the child or another member of the family. Anticonvulsants, analgesics, hypnotics, and tranquillisers are particularly common. In contrast with accidental poisoning, deliberate poisoning is often recurrent and may involve more than one drug (Fig. 9.1).

It is important to be aware that a parent, usually the mother, may have poisoned the child. The story should always be checked carefully for credibility – could such a young child have had access to those particular tablets? Accidental ingestion of a pill, or any small foreign body, is unlikely under the age of 12 months. Two year old children probably cannot reach the top shelf of a high kitchen cupboard nor can they unwrap individually foil packed tablets or open child resistant containers. Child resistant containers are not child proof, but they do delay access to the contents; when in doubt about the child's manipulative skills or development, it is worth playing with the child to test their ability to pick up a small object or to open a container or pack of the type described by the parent.

Presentations of non-accidental poisoning

Intentional poisoning is commonest in children below the age of 3 but may occur at any age. Children who have been poisoned by a parent are likely to present in four main ways.
- Alleged accidental ingestion
- Unusual or inexplicable symptoms and signs, usually of acute onset, with little or no history of preceding illness
- Recurrent unexplained illnesses – for example, recurrent episodes of drowsiness or hyperventilation. These sorts of patients overlap

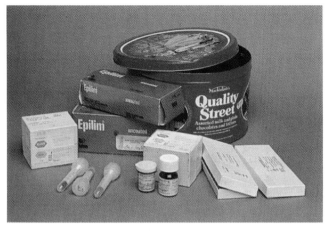

Figure 9.1 A 3 year old presented with recurrent seizures that did not respond to the usual anticonvulsants. She began to develop recurrent bouts of drowsiness. At first the mother denied giving her drugs inappropriately but subsequently displayed them together with the container in which they were kept. When separated from her mother the child no longer had "seizures".

with those for whom parents create false illness (fabricated or induced illness) by other means
* The child may be moribund or dead when first seen by the doctor.

Motive

A two year survey of non-accidental poisoning in the British Isles showed that two thirds of the cases occurred in the context of illness in the child fabricated or induced by the mother. The other third occurred for various reasons, including parents seeking to "teach their child a lesson"; those who were themselves addicted to drugs, such as methadone or cannabis, and involved the child from an early age; and mothers who gave the child a drug to stop crying or enforce sleep.

Establishing poisoning

Identifying poisoning can be difficult, even when the doctor is alert to the possibility (Table 9.2). Most hospitals have limited biochemi-

---

Box 9.1 **Salt poisoning**

* A notorious poison given by carers is table salt – sodium chloride (NaCl). Strong salt solutions are unpleasant and nauseating, which limits the amount that can be taken; the infant is usually given excess salt and deprived of water; incurring hypernatraemia *and* dehydration. Salt can be put into a gastrostomy or intravenous line. Hypernatraemia develops leading to irritation, seizures, and coma. Death may occur.
* Deliberate salt poisoning is often recurrent and associated with much higher serum sodium concentrations – for example, 180 mmol/l – than occur in natural disorders. The high concentrations of serum sodium and chloride are associated with high concentrations in the urine. Quantitative analysis of urine samples collected over a prolonged period provides the best proof of poisoning. Hypernatraemia may lead to a confusing hyperglycaemia.

Table 9.2 Presentation of poisoning

Symptoms/signs	Drug
Seizures and apnoeic spells	• Phenothiazines • Tricyclic antidepressants • Hydrocarbons • Lignocaine • Salt (sodium chloride) (Box 9.1)
Hyperventilation	• Salicylates • Acids
Drowsiness and stupor, encephalopathy	• Anticonvulsants • Hypnotics • Insulin • Analgesics • Tricylic antidepressants • Phenothiazines • Methadone and cannabis
Hallucinations	• Atropine-like agents
Agitation, tachycardia	• Amphetamines
Bizarre motor movements (myoclonic jerks, tremors, extrapyramidal signs)	• Phenothiazines • Metoclopramide • Antihistamines
Vomiting	• Emetics and many other drugs
Diarrhoea (with or without failure to thrive)	• Laxatives • Salt
Haematemesis	• Salicylates • Iron
Ulcerated mouth	• Corrosives
Thirst	• Salt • Amphetamines • Lithium
Bizarre biochemical blood profile	• Salt • Insulin • Salicylates • Sodium bicarbonate • Water intoxication

cal screening facilities, confined to screening for major common drugs in urine samples; there is no fully comprehensive toxicology screen available. Doctors should:
* Think of possible drugs responsible for the child's symptoms
* Try to identify from the general practitioner or hospital records any drugs that might be present in the household or to which the parent or carer has access
* Ask the laboratory to look specifically for that drug in the child's urine or blood.

It is important to ask the laboratory to explain the limitations of their tests, which are often considerable; and it is worth finding out if the parents' jobs give them access to particular drugs – for example, if a parent is a health professional or works in a hospital. Until such information is available samples of urine, blood, vomit, and faeces should be kept safely in the refrigerator. Electrolyte measurements of the stool are useful in identifying secretory diarrhoea (Na >75 mmol/l) resulting from stimulant laxatives. Some tablets and capsules are radio-opaque and can show on x ray pictures if they are taken within a few hours of the child ingesting the tablets.

It is particularly important to preserve samples of urine, blood, and tissues when a child is brought in moribund with apparent encephalopathy, liver failure, bleeding disorder, or bizarre biochemical results. Urine is usually the most useful sample and should be obtained if necessary by catheterisation or suprapubic aspiration. When such children die the coroner must be informed. Whenever there is a strong suspicion of poisoning the police should also be informed.

Initially it is more important to identify the drug than the method by which it has been given. The methods are sometimes so bizarre that they defy commonsense reasoning. A determined parent or carer can find ways of poisoning a child, even under close supervision with the child in hospital. Carers have injected insulin into intravenous lines, poured medicine into gastrostomy tubes, put nasogastric tubes down into the child's stomach to administer particularly noxious solutions that the child would not otherwise take, and secreted tablets in their mouth that they have passed on to the child with a kiss. Rectal administration has also been used. Identify the poison first and only then start investigating how the child was given it.

If poisoning is suspected the parent should be given every chance to explain how it happened. Dispensing errors are possible; mistakes are made. Many parents give drugs, tonics, and traditional remedies to their child. Some are fearful of discussing it because they think the doctor would disapprove; others are embarrassed at using a rather naive remedy for their child. Doctors should sympathetically explore with the parent the ways in which a child might have ingested a particular poison. This is particularly important for people from unconventional backgrounds or from different ethnic cultures, who may use many different sources of health advice.

Further reading

American Academy of Pediatrics Committee on Drugs. Transfer of drugs and other chemicals into human milk. *Pediatrics* 1994;93:137–50.

Bays J, Feldman KW. Child abuse by poisoning. In: Reece RM, Ludwig S, eds. *Child abuse: medical diagnosis and management*. Philadelphia, PA: Lippincott Williams & Wilkins, 2001:405–41.

McClure RJ, Davis PM, Meadow SR, Sibert JR. Epidemiology of Munchausen syndrome by proxy, non-accidental poisoning, and non-accidental suffocation. *Arch Dis Child* 1996;75:57–61.

Meadow R. Non-accidental salt poisoning. *Arch Dis Child* 1993;68:448–52.

Toxbase: www.spib.axl.co.uk

CHAPTER 10

Fatal Abuse and Smothering

Roy Meadow

Figure 10.1 Despite the publicity given in the past 20 years to violence and murder of elderly women, police officers, and ethnic minorities, the person most at risk remains the infant – by parental action.

Many forms of child abuse may lead to the death of the child. Physical abuse is the commonest reason. Head injuries are an important cause of death as a result of a young child being shaken, hit, or hurled. Visceral injuries, though uncommon, have a disproportionately high mortality. For all these injuries, a misleading history and delay in presentation to doctors interfere with optimal treatment. Death also occurs from severe burning, drowning, poisoning, starvation,

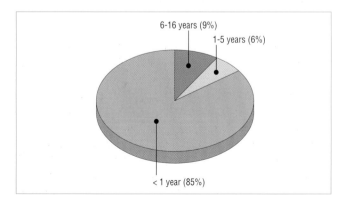

Figure 10.2 Child homicides, England and Wales 1990–2002, by age.

and neglect. Research suggests that the number of deaths from abuse has decreased in the past 20 years, mainly because of the work of child protection agencies and better medical care.

Age of victim

Nearly all the fatalities occur in children below the age of 5 and most in infants (age below a year) (Fig. 10.2). One reason is that infants are less robust and therefore more vulnerable to physical injury; they can neither defend themselves against attack nor fend for themselves if neglected. US surveys suggest that about 4% of infants incurring physical abuse die.

Perpetrator

When a child is killed the usual perpetrator is the child's parent or carer. The homicide occurs at home. Collusion between two parents is unsusual. The killing of a child by a parent or step-parent is sometimes called filicide.

Though parents worry about their child being attacked or murdered by a stranger, and such events achieve massive publicity, they are rare. Similarly the well publicised family annihilator who kills himself, his partner, and his children is also rare.

Circumstances

The reasons for the killing range from those in which there is no intention to kill or harm and impulsive violence, to those in which the parent views the child with anger or jealousy, the parent with ill founded ideas of discipline, and those with frank psychosis. The younger the infant the more likely it is that the mother is responsible. Fatal poisoning and smothering are much more likely to be perpetrated by the mother than the father.

> **Homicide (murder, manslaughter, and infanticide)**
> **The risk of homicide in the first year of life is greater than in any other year**

Most parents who kill are not found to have mental illness when subject to expert assessment by psychiatrists. Many have personality disorders and have reacted fatally to difficult circumstances, including poverty, lack of supporting family and friends, and the demands of awkward children. If the parent comes from a background of family violence or there is drug or alcohol dependence the risks are greater.

Recognition

Deaths that result from major physical abuse and the extreme end of most forms of child abuse are rarely difficult to diagnose. But a much more difficult subject is covert killing, for instance by smothering, in which a young child dies suddenly with few, or no, abnormal signs. In recent years there has been greater recognition of this occurrence and a willingness to confront the issue of unrecognised fatal child abuse. The difficulty lies in doing so in a way that is sensitive to the feelings of parents who suffer the tragedy of a young child dying, suddenly and unexpectedly, from natural causes.

> Legal definition of infanticide:
> The killing of a child under the age of 12 months by the child's mother "when the balance of her mind was disturbed because she had not fully recovered from the effect of child birth or lactation"

Sudden infant death syndrome (SIDS)

The label of sudden infant death is used when a previously well infant dies suddenly and unexpectedly and neither the preceding history nor the autopsy results suggest a cause of death. It is reached by a process of exclusion and means that the cause of death is not known. The term should not be used unless there has been a careful investigation of the death scene, a full autopsy by an experienced pathologist including skeletal survey and toxicology, and careful review of all medical and social service records by a paediatrician. Ideally that should be followed by a case discussion between all the professionals involved. The campaigns to improve safe conditions

---

Box 10.1 **Warning features that sudden infant death may have been caused by smothering**

History
- Previous acute life threatening event or unexplained apnoea/seizures/cyanosis, occurring only in the care of the same person
- Previous unusual disorders or injuries
- Previous unexplained disorders affecting siblings
- Other unexplained deaths of children in the family

Secondary features:
- An excess of unusual illnesses during the mother's pregnancy
- Open warning – a mother who predicted the death of the child
- Death within 36 hours of being discharged well from hospital
- Death within short interval of taking normal feed
- Unusual response to event – for example, failure to dial 999 or seek help
- Unusual response after the death – for example, bizarre mourning rituals

Examination
- Bruises, petechiae
- Frank blood on face, in nose or mouth

Autopsy
- Rib fractures or other injury unlikely to be result of resuscitation
- Fresh blood in airways, old blood (haemosiderin) in alveoli
- Paper/fabric tissue or other foreign bodies in the gut or airways

---

for young children, including putting the infant to sleep supine, appropriate bedding, and avoiding overheating and smoking, as well as advances in the early detection of illness, have contributed to a decline in the numbers of babies dying unexpectedly. Nevertheless, SIDS is an important category of death in Britain, accounting for nearly 10% of deaths in the first year of life. Ninety per cent of the deaths occur before the age of six months. Many different causes, some in combination, are likely to be responsible. Epidemiological and twin studies suggest that, in general, adverse social and environmental factors are much more important than genetic factors. Recurrence within a family is uncommon (see reviews by Hunt 2001, Reece 2001, and Getahun D, et al 2004)

It has long been recognised that a small proportion of sudden unexpected deaths in infancy are the result of a parent's actions (acts of commission as well as omission). As many of the natural causes of infant deaths have been eliminated and mortality has fallen, the proportion caused by parents is likely to have increased gradually. Some deaths are caused by deliberate acts such as suffocation, others result from poor care and neglect that may or may not be deliberate. It is not possible to know the proportion of sudden unexpected deaths in infancy that result from parental action.

Smothering

Asphyxia is an uncommon but serious form of child abuse (Box 10.1). If brief it may merely be a terrifying ordeal for the child. If the period of brain hypoxia is prolonged, however, permanent brain damage or death may result. The commonest method is by smothering (imposed upper airway obstruction); the abuser, usually the parent, uses a hand, pillow, or pad of clothing to cause mechanical obstruction of the child's airways. Less commonly the abuser presses the child's face against his or her chest, uses a plastic bag, or presses on the child's neck.

> Smothering is commonest under the age of 1 and rare over the age of 3. The usual perpetrator is the mother rather than the father

Clinical features

The infant presents to doctors either as a sudden unexplained death, moribund, or as a single or recurrent episode of being found cyanotic, floppy, and having stopped breathing. An acute life threatening event (ALTE) is one in which there is objective evidence of an event, such as an experienced third party witness or confirmatory physical findings. The mother's account usually leads doctors to diagnose an apnoeic attack or a seizure. (If a mother describes a young baby as having stopped breathing or having seemed unconscious for a short time the doctor usually calls it an apnoeic attack whereas in an older child the same description is likely to be considered a seizure.) For some children the smothering is associated with other forms of abuse. The British Isles survey into the incidence of suffocation identified mainly the severe and repetitive cases and found that half of those occurred in the context of fabricated or induced illness, the child being presented to doctors repeatedly because of apnoea or collapses. When such an infant is being presented repetitively be-

Figure 10.3 Petechial haemorrhage at 3 o' clock. Similar haemorrhages were present on the upper cheeks of this child who survived smothering.

cause of "stopping breathing" there is usually a mixture of events, some of which are merely false stories, and others that have been caused by smothering and may have led to experienced observers finding the infant blue or lifeless. Single acts of smothering, even if fatal, are unlikely to be detected. Infants make a speedy recovery from brief episodes of asphyxia, compared with the slower recovery that may follow seizures and metabolic upsets.

Those providing a highly specialised service for children with alleged recurrent apnoea and sleep apnoea and who issue monitoring equipment to such families are likely to encounter children incurring repetitive smothering. Firstman and Talan have described the medical confusion initially linking recurrent apnoea with infant deaths, and the later revelation of serial killers of three, or even nine, children.

Signs

Smothering is violent: a young child who cannot breathe struggles and tries to get air. Characteristically the adult lays the child on his or her back, or against something firm, so that the hand or cushion may

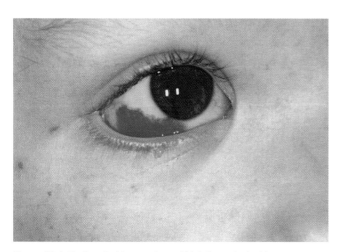

Figure 10.4 Conjunctival haemorrhage. This infant who had been smothered also had bleeding from the nose.

be held hard against the face. An arm is used to restrain struggling limbs. The smothering probably has to persist for at least a minute to cause seizures, longer to cause brain damage, and over two minutes to cause death. (Damage may be more sudden if the child, as a result of the assault, has a cardiac arrest or vomits and chokes.) Despite the violence entailed, signs may be non-existent or few. Hand pressure sometimes leaves thumb marks or fingerprints around the nose or mouth or abrasions inside the mouth with bruising of the gums. Sometimes the asphyxiation leads to multiple petechiae on the face, particularly on the eyelids and conjunctiva (Figs 10.3 and 10.4), as a result of intravascular pressure, lack of oxygen, and retention of carbon dioxide. Bleeding from the mucous membranes of the nose or mouth (frank blood rather than pinkish froth) is an important positive finding in a minority of cases. Examination inside the nose and mouth with an otoscope may reveal the source. Immediately after a bout of severe hypoxia the infant commonly has an increased respiratory rate and non-specific signs of extreme stress such as hyperglycaemia and raised white cell count. Chest x ray pictures may show pulmonary oedema. Usually recovery to normal is rapid.

Fatal smothering may be associated with no external signs, and at autopsy there may be no specific signs that enable experienced forensic or paediatric pathologists to differentiate smothering from other SIDS. Some of the children who have suffered recurrent bouts of smothering have evidence of previous bleeding into the lungs and an excess of haemosiderin-laden macrophages in the alveoli. Some may have more specific evidence of brain damage from anoxia, but most will not have specific pathological evidence of smothering. Thus, there has to be careful exploration of all the circumstances and previous history when the cause of death is considered.

Differential diagnosis

Unexplained episodes suggesting apnoea or possible seizures are commonly reported by mothers of young babies. Sometimes an anxious mother perceives illness that is not there, or overinterprets the periodic breathing and normal movements of a healthy baby. Therefore in all such cases it is worth seeking a description of the episodes from another relative. This is particularly important if the mother is suspected of causing them.

True apnoea, in which the breathing stops for 20 seconds or more and is followed by bradycardia, cyanosis, or pallor, is frightening and often unexplained. It is more likely in small preterm infants and usually starts in the neonatal period. In early life both respiratory syncytial virus infection and whooping cough can be associated with spells of apnoea in previously well infants; the apnoea may precede the cough or other respiratory signs by a few days.

Whenever apnoea starts unexpectedly in a previously well baby it must be investigated thoroughly. The investigations should include careful checks for cardiac, respiratory, or seizure disorder, oesophageal reflux, and biochemical abnormality. When these investigations give normal results consideration should be given to whether the episodes are caused by the parent; if the episodes are frequent, a period in hospital without the parent might be the wisest course. If severe episodes are frequent at home and absent in hospital away from the parent, the parent is probably responsible. Video surveillance of the infant and parent in hospital can be a highly specific diagnostic test: filmed evidence of suffocation provides conclusive proof. But its sensitivity is unsure as most abuse occurs at home and the parent may not abuse the child during the short period of video surveillance in hospital. The surveillance is done by the police, after a decision made at a multi-agency strategy discussion, according to guidelines from the Department of Health.

Further reading

AAP Committee on Child Abuse and Neglect. Distinguishing sudden infant death syndrome from child abuse fatalities. *Pediatrics* 2006;118:421–7.

Department of Health. Safeguarding children in whom illness is fabricated or induced. London: DoH, 2002.

Firstman R, Talan J. *The death of innocents*. London: Bantam, 1998.

Fleming P, Blair P, Bacon C, Berry J, eds. *Sudden unexpected deaths in infancy*. London: Stationery Office, 2000.

Getahun D, Demissie K, Shou-En L, Rhoade GG. Sudden infant death syndrome among twin births, United States, 1995–8. *J Perinatol* 2004;24:544–51.

Hunt CE. Recurrence risk for sudden death. *Am J Resp Crit Care Med* 2001;164:346–57.

Meadow R. Unnatural sudden infant death. *Arch Dis Child* 1999;80:7–14.

NSPCC. *Out of sight: report on child deaths from abuse*. 2nd ed. London: NSPCC, 2001.

Reece RM, Ludwig S, eds. Fatal child abuse and sudden infant death syndrome. *Child abuse: medical diagnosis and management*. Philadelphia, PA: Lippincott, Williams & Wilkins, 2001: 517–43.

Royal College of Pathologists, and Royal College of Paediatrics and Child Health. *Sudden unexpected death in infancy: a multi agency protocol for care and investigation*. London: Royal College of Pathologists/Royal College of Paediatrics and Child Health, 2004.

Southall DP, Plunkett BM, Banks MW, Falkov AF, Samuels MP. Covert video recordings of life-threatening child abuse: Lessons for child protection. *Pediatr* 1997;100:735–59.

Wilczynski A. *Child homicide*. Glasgow: Bell and Bain, 1997.

CHAPTER 11

Child Sexual Abuse: The Problem

Christopher Hobbs

Table 11.1 Relative commonness of childhood conditions, US

Condition	Incidence during childhood
Sexual abuse	20% girls, 9% boys
Otitis media	70%
Syncope	15%
Asthma	10–12%
Diabetes	0.25%
Cancer	0.1%
Sickle cell disease	0.25% of black children

Child sexual abuse has threatened political, religious, and cultural institutions and dominated newspaper coverage in many countries for days and weeks at a time. It has divided families, friends, and communities. Its importance is enormous and yet, apart from infrequent citings of seismic proportions, it remains for the most part hidden in the shadow of secrecy. Society on the one hand rejects and stigmatises the behaviour, while on the other it ignores and denies it. No society condones it. While anthropologists have theorised about the universality of the taboo of incest, suggesting the rarity of actual incest, the cultural reality has been the presence of widespread incest and child molestation in most places at most times (Table 11.1, Figs 11.1 and 11.2).

In ancient history the code of Hammurabi (2150 BC) stated that "If a man be known to his daughter, they shall expel that man from the city." Descriptions of the use of children for sex can be found in the literature of ancient Greece and Rome. Anal intercourse with boys was prevalent. There is more recent historic evidence of child sexual abuse. Ambroise Tardieu, an important figure in forensic circles in Europe in 1858–69 cited 11 576 people accused of completed or attempted rape in France. More than nine thousand of the victims were children, mostly girls aged between 4 and 12 years. Freud described his patients' histories of childhood sexual abuse, though later explained them away as fantasy.

Definition

The sexual exploitation of children is the involvement of dependent, developmentally immature children and adolescents in sexual activities that they do not fully comprehend and are unable to give informed consent to and that violate the social taboos of family roles.

Epidemiology

Child sexual abuse occurs in children of all ages, including the very young. It happens to both boys and girls. It occurs in all classes of society, most commonly within the privacy of the family. It is impossible to know the true prevalence, but there are many indicators that the practice is widespread.

- Nineteen per cent of 2869 young UK adults said they had been sexually abused as a child: 1% reported abuse by parents or carers, 3% by other relatives, 11% by known but unrelated people, and 4% by strangers
- In a UK student sample 50% of young women and 25% of young men had some form of sexually abusive experience, with or without physical contact, before the age of 18
- An estimated 100 000 children are exposed to potentially harmful sexual experiences every year in the UK
- Over a period of six to eight months the British Crime Survey estimated that 1 in 10 girls aged 12 to 15 had been sexually harassed by adult men. One in 50 boys had a similar experience. Half the victims had been very frightened
- Sexual abuse of children occurs worldwide and is independent of the wealth or poverty of the nation
- Sexually abusive behaviour is usually repetitive, with one or many victims
- Around 50–75% of victims incur repetitive abuse. A child who has been sexually abused is at risk of further abuse by the same, or a different, perpetrator.

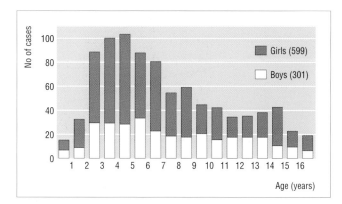

Figure 11.1 Distribution of 900 children diagnosed in Leeds (population ≈ 750,000), 1986–8, by sex and age. (Data from Hobbs *et al.* 1999.)

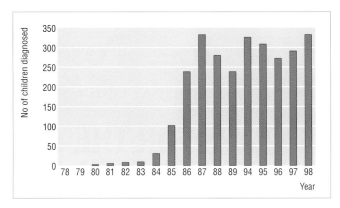

Figure 11.2 Sexually abused children diagnosed by paediatricians in Leeds. Note the rapid rise in cases in the early 1980s that followed increased recognition. A slight dip followed the Cleveland inquiry, but numbers remained high in the years where records were complete, up to 1998.

Which children are abused?

Studies have shown that girls report child sexual abuse more commonly than boys do. Boys disclose abuse less often and the abuse is more likely to be overlooked. The age range for such abuse is from infancy to adolescence. Some children are more vulnerable. These include children with disabilities; neglected children; those looked after ("in care"); and children whose biological parents are separated (the abuser may be a parent, step parent, or other).

Context of abuse

Intrafamilial abuse includes abuse within the nuclear and extended family or adoptive and foster family (Fig. 11.3).

Close acquaintances – abusers can be neighbours, family friends, or parents of school friends, and abuse within "sex rings." In sex rings, groups of children are organised around a paedophile who lives locally. Children visit the adult for a soft drink, small monetary gifts, and attention. In return they are groomed, sworn to secrecy, and abused.

Institutional abuse occurs within schools, residential children's establishments, day nurseries, and holiday camps and in sporting, social, and other community organisations, both secular and religious. Street or stranger abuse includes assaults on children in public places, including child abduction. This context of child sexual abuse is less common, but individual cases tend to generate much publicity. The internet offers paedophiles a unique opportunity to target, groom, and abuse children in secrecy in their homes. Recent high profile cases have confirmed that new strategies must be developed to counter what has already become a reality, and not just a theoretical possibility. These different contexts are not mutually exclusive. Some children are abused in several contexts.

Types of abuse – contact or non-contact

Contact abuse

- Contact abuse involves touching, fondling, and oral or genital contact with the child's breast, genitals, or anus
- Masturbation may be by an adult of him/herself in the presence of the child, including ejaculation on to the child, by adult of child, or by child of adult
- Penetration may be insertion of fingers or objects into the vulva or anus. Intercourse is vaginal, anal, or oral, whether actual or attempted in any degree. This is usually with the adult as the active party but in some cases a child may be encouraged to penetrate the adult (Fig. 11.4)
- Rape is attempted or achieved penile penetration of the vagina. Other genital contact includes intercrural intercourse, where the penis is laid between the legs, or genital contact with any part of the child's body – for example, a penis rubbed on a child's thigh
- Prostitution involves any of the above forms of abuse that includes the exchange of money, gifts, or favours and applies to both boys ("rent boys") and girls
- Sadistic sexual activities – for example, ligatures, restraints, and various mutilation.

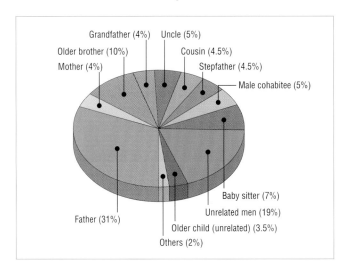

Figure 11.3 Relationship of perpetrator to child in 337 cases of child sexual abuse diagnosed in Leeds, 1985–6. Adapted from Hobbs CJ, Wynne JM. *Lancet* 1987;II:837–41.

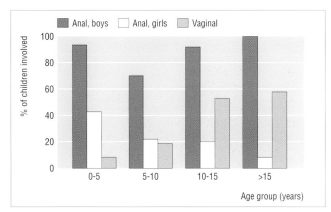

Figure 11.4 Proportion of children by age and sex who gave a history or had signs of anal or vaginal penetration in the Leeds sexual abuse study. Adapted from Hobbs CJ, Wynne JM. *Child abuse and neglect* 1989;13:195–210.

Figure 11.6 Newspaper report of the prosecution of a deputy head teacher for the abuse of children with moderate learning difficulties.

Non-contact abuse

- Non-contact abuse involves exhibitionism (flashing), pornography (photographing sexual acts or anatomy), showing pornographic images (photographs, films, videos), and erotic talk (telling children titillating or sexually explicit stories)
- Accessing child pornography – for example, via the internet – is also abuse (Box 11.1). This is now more commonly recognised and perpetrators are prosecuted more often.

Links with other forms of abuse

Physical abuse and child sexual abuse are closely related (Fig. 11.5). One in six physically abused children is sexually abused. One in seven sexually abused children is also physically abused. Physically abused children must therefore be assessed for sexual abuse. Patterns of injury that may suggest child sexual abuse include:

- Sadistic injury
- Injuries around genital area, lower abdomen, or breasts
- Restraint type injuries (grips or ligature marks to buttocks, thighs, knees, ankles, arms, or neck)
- Some bites – for example, love bites.

Severe and fatal physical abuse may be associated with sexual abuse. This may occur when the abuser acts to terrorise or silence the child. Neglected children suffer higher levels of sexual abuse. All forms of sexual abuse involve some emotional abuse.

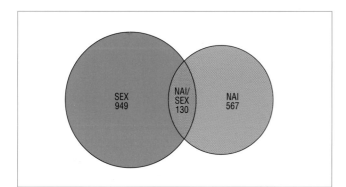

Figure 11.5 Overlap of physical and sexual abuse (NAI=non-accidental injury). (Data from Hobbs & Wynne 1990.)

Perpetrators of child sexual abuse and paedophilia

Perpetrators include men and women. Twenty five percent are teenagers of either sex. Sexually abusive behaviour often starts in late childhood and adolescence. Many perpetrators were abused or neglected as children. Abused children who as adults go on to abuse other children are more likely to have grown up in a climate of violence and a pattern of insecure care.

Some child sexual abuse occurs outside the family. A paedophile is someone who has an exclusive or predominant sexual interest in children. He or she may:

- Actively seek out children through work or other activities that bring regular contact. A man may target single women with children and become involved in the child care
- Abuse children for years undetected – for example, a deputy head in a school for children with moderate learning difficulties abused children for 20 years (Fig. 11.6)
- Be "child wise" and use a sense of the child's needs and vulnerability to access, lure, groom, and abuse children so as to escape detection and prosecution (often viewed as "well thought of and relating well with children")
- Have an age or sex specific interest in children – for example, teenage girls or prepubescent boys
- Abuse many children and, when convicted, may provide details of several hundred child victims
- Use false names or aliases, gain access to children by deceit, and exploit loopholes in the system to protect children. Paedophiles often avoid detection by frightening and intimidating their victims into silence.

Once convicted, paedophiles can be tracked through the sex offenders register (Box 11.2).

Consequences of sexual abuse

The consequences of sexual abuse include immediate and long term effects. They range from acquiring a sexually transmitted infection, becoming pregnant, or experiencing violence or murder to the variable psychological and emotional effects that together account for most of the morbidity (Table 11.2, Fig. 11.7). The effects stretch into adult life with problems in relationships, social functioning, sexual-

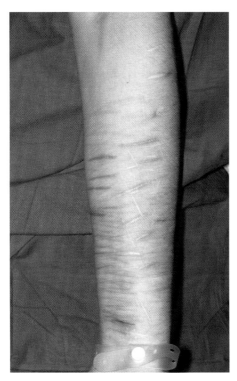

Figure 11.7 Self inflicted razor cut marks on a distressed teenage girl.

Table 11.2 Incidence of problems in sexually abused children

Problem	% of children
Educational problems	
All	24
Statement of special educational need	16
Adverse behaviours	
All	60
Aggressive behaviour	22
Sexualised behaviour	19
Chronic health problems	
All	54
Soiling	10
Wetting	20
Abnormal growth patterns	18
Involvement of mental health services	32
Further abuse after original diagnosis	
All	35
Social disruption	
In care of local authority or adopted	25
Surname change	30
Increase in number of schools attended	Twice the average

ity, and child rearing. One in three adults (3% of the total population) who were sexually abused as children reports a lasting and permanent effect. Increased frequency of a history of child sexual abuse has been associated with such diverse conditions as anorexia nervosa and irritable bowel syndrome. There are also links with various psychiatric disorders including post-traumatic stress disorder and depression. The incidence of child sexual abuse is higher in women who turn to prostitution. Additionally, there are important associations with criminality.

The idea that suppressed memories of child sexual abuse can be reactivated by psychological therapies is challenged in the "false memory syndrome," where it is claimed that false memories have been implanted by the therapist.

The consequences of sexual abuse have been the subject of substantial study. There have been few studies of medically diagnosed groups, however, in which most participants had been abused within a family.

Sexually abused children aged 7 or less at the time of abuse have been followed up through school health records. High levels of morbidity were found in children up to 8 years after the abuse was diagnosed. Compared with children in a control group, social, educational, and health problems left many children substantially disadvantaged.

Prevention

Efforts to prevent child sexual abuse have concentrated on strengthening children's awareness and ability to keep themselves safe from the control of known offenders. There is little evidence with which

---

Box 11.2 Sex offender orders

These orders, made where necessary for public protection, last for any period from five years or "until further notice." They require the person named to be subject to notification under the Sex Offenders Act 1997, and prohibit any actions specified by the order.

Schedule 1 offenders
People convicted of an offence specified in schedule 1 of the Children and Young Persons Act 1933 (as amended by subsequent legislation) are sometimes referred to as "schedule 1 offenders." These offences include murder, manslaughter, and other forms of violence or bodily injury against children and young people, and also specified sexual offences against children and young people. Schedule 1 offenders are subject to specific child protection provisions and, if this is shown in the course of police checks, may impact on the decisions as to their suitability to care for, or work with, children and young people.

---

to measure the success of these limited interventions. Despite this, the numbers of cases identified recently in both the US and UK have been falling. It is not clear whether this is evidence of success or failure to address the problem.

Further reading

Browne KD, Hanks HGI, Stratton P, Hamilton C. *Early prediction and prevention of child abuse and neglect*. Chichester: Wiley, 2002.

Butler-Sloss E. *Report of the inquiry into child abuse in Cleveland 1987*. London: HMSO, 1988.

Cawson P, Wattam C, Brooker S, Kelly G. *Child maltreatment in the United Kingdom. A study of the prevalence of child abuse and neglect*. London: NSPCC, 2000.

De Mause L. *The history of childhood*. London: Souvenir Press, 1980.

Finkelhor D. The international epidemiology of child sexual abuse. *Child Abuse Neglect* 1994;18:409–17.

Frothingham TE, Hobbs CJ, Wynne JM, Goyal A, Dobbs J, Yee L, et al. Follow-up study eight years after diagnosis of sexual abuse. *Arch Dis Child* 2002;82:132–4.

Hobbs CJ, Wynne JM. The sexually abused battered child. *Arch Dis Child* 1990;65:423–7.

Hobbs CJ, Hanks H, Wynne JM. *Child abuse and neglect*. New York: Churchill Livingstone, 1999.

Holmes WC, Slap GB. Sexual abuse of boys: definition, prevalence, correlates, sequelae, and management. *JAMA* 1998;280:1855–62.

Johnson CF. Child sexual abuse. *Lancet* 2004;364:462–70.

CHAPTER 12

Child Sexual Abuse: Clinical Approach

Christopher Hobbs

Medical assessment

This term medical assessment is preferable to medical examination because the emphasis is on assessment of the whole child rather than just genital or anal examination. The doctor, usually a paediatrician, brings knowledge and understanding of children and child development to this assessment.

The doctor will take a full history and carry out a physical examination; assess any injury; assess any abuse; collect any forensic evidence (includes proper documentation of "physical signs" associated with abuse); help with the process of (psychological) healing; and arrange for referral or treatment for any consequences of the abuse – for example, sexually transmitted disease, pregnancy, psychological trauma (Fig. 12.1).

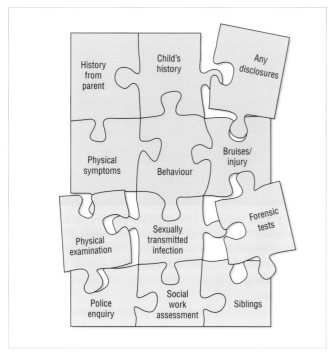

Figure 12.1 The jigsaw of abuse. Adapted from Hobbs C, et al. *Child abuse and neglect. A clinician's handbook.* 2nd ed. New York: Churchill Livingstone, 1999.

Presentation of child sexual abuse

Child sexual abuse presents in many ways, some of which may be initiated by a family member or other adult.

Disclosure

Disclosure describes the gradual process by which a child tells of his or her predicament. Around 5% of children tell an adult in authority about the abuse but more tell a friend. Children prefer to tell someone they trust and believe will protect them. However, most keep it a secret, under threats of one form or another.

Abuse in the home can be accommodated for years, resulting in delayed and unconvincing disclosure followed by swift retraction. False allegations are uncommon, ranging from 0.5% to 8% of cases, with higher figures occurring in the course of custody and contact disputes. Some children, however, are encouraged or coached into naming someone who has not abused them.

Children's statements should be heard and documented (Box 12.1). They are tested out in investigative interviews undertaken by appropriately trained staff from police and social services to agreed practice standards ("Memorandum of Good Practice"). Communicating with and listening to children requires skill and sensitivity as well as the ability to read children's messages. Drawings and play may be particularly useful in enabling communication. Interviews are usually recorded by video or audiotape for possible use as evidence in criminal or care proceedings. Inappropriate questioning of the child – for example, by the use of leading or suggestive questioning – could contaminate verbal evidence and must be avoided.

Concerning signs and symptoms

Children may present with:

- General medical and social history
- Bowel and urinary history
- Sexual and menstrual history
- History of genital or anal symptoms
- Behaviour changes
- Developmental history.

If the police and social services have already interviewed the child fully, check the history with them; only essential details need to be confirmed with the child. If no interview has taken place more history will be needed and this should be taken by allowing the child to speak freely, avoiding leading questions, and keeping a careful verbatim account of both questions and answers. Anything disclosed by the child may form evidence in court. Inappropriate direct and leading questions may introduce information or contaminate this evidence.

When to examine a child's genitals and anus

Examination of the anogenital area of a child should be part of the routine examination. It is essential in many clinical situations – for example, with urinary infection, soiling, abdominal pain. It is wise to seek specific (additional) consent for this part of the examination from the child and parent.

The medical examination for suspected sexual abuse requires a doctor with specific expertise and training; facilities for the use of the colposcope (Fig. 12.6) and photographic documentation; and knowledge of sexually transmitted infection and appropriate forensic testing. When contact abuse is thought to have taken place recently, consideration must be given, in conjunction with the police, to obtaining forensic samples that could assist in identifying the perpetrator. Positive samples of semen are obtained more often from objects such as furniture or carpets than from swabs taken from the child. Guidance on paediatric forensic examinations in relation to possible child sexual abuse is contained in the joint statement of the Royal College of Paediatrics and Child Health and the Association of forensic physicians.

- Examination in the prepubertal child is inspection only
- In postpubertal girls labial separation and gentle labial traction are usually needed to display the hymen and opening. Assessment of the diameter of the hymenal opening may be helped by gentle insertion of a finger (Figs 12.7 and 12.8)
- In pubertal girls, a speculum examination may be possible to assist further sampling
- Anal inspection is usually performed in the left lateral position; if a different position is used it is noted. Part the buttocks, observe for 30 seconds, as there may be a delay before the anus dilates. Veins may also fill slowly.

Examination findings in child sexual abuse

- Abnormality is found in less than half the children examined because of possible sexual abuse, while diagnostic findings are present in only a small minority
- Normality does not equate with "no abuse"
- Physical signs "supportive of sexual abuse" may corroborate the child's history
- Physical signs can be caused by trauma (rubbing, stretching, blunt trauma) or infection, or both

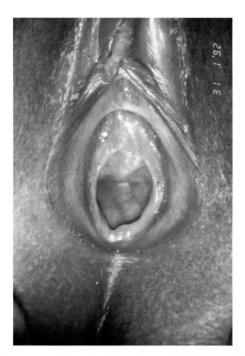

Figure 12.7 Attenuated hymen with notch posteriorly in 9 year old who disclosed penetrative abuse by an uncle.

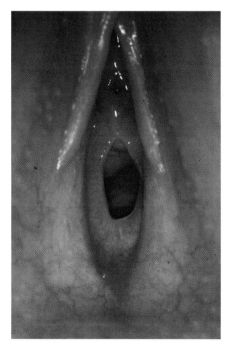

Figure 12.8 Normal annular hymen in a 6 year old girl.

- Healing is often rapid and scars are uncommon
- Follow-up examination is useful in evaluating physical signs, excluding organic disease, and recognising healing or further abuse
- Signs depend on type, frequency, and force of abuse. The age of the child and the time since the last episode of abuse also affect the presence of signs

- Diagnosis of sexual abuse is usually made by consideration of all factors rather than on a single sign.

Sexually transmitted infection (STI)

The paediatrician may, as a coincidental finding, be presented with a positive result for a sexually transmitted infection in a child in whom sexual abuse has not been suspected. The relevance of the infection depends on the organism and needs careful interpretation. Advice should be sought from a consultant in genitourinary medicine. The result should be discussed with the parent or carer, and a history obtained on the social and family circumstances, including the possibility of sexual abuse. If other modes of acquisition have been excluded and if risk factors are identified an inter-agency discussion should follow to gather information and plan further investigations.

As child sexual abuse is increasingly recognised, so is the presence of sexually transmitted infection and its importance. In all children who may have been sexually abused, the risk of such infection should be considered.

- Mode of transmission can be via the mother (transplacental or perinatal, particularly chlamydia and human papilloma virus) or injecting drug use or blood products, sexual, or accidental (fomite, close physical contact, or autoinoculation), which is exceptionally uncommon
- Sexually transmitted infection may provide conclusive evidence of abuse – for example, when the same infection is identified in the alleged perpetrator and the child and other sources of infection have been excluded (for example, perinatal from the mother). The scope and the limitations of the diagnostic test should be discussed with the laboratory involved

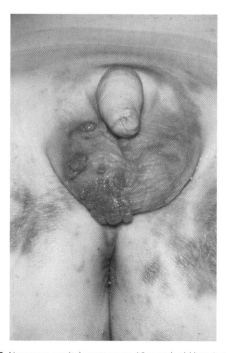

Figure 12.9 Numerous genital warts on an 18 month old boy. In this case the mode of transmission was uncertain.

Figure 12.10 This 3 year old complained of sore genitals. The eggs (nits) of pubic lice can be seen adhering to her eyelashes.

- The risk of infection depends on the age of the child, the mechanism of abuse, and the population prevalence of sexually transmitted infection
- Important infections include chlamydia, human papilloma virus, herpes simplex virus, *Trichomonas*, HIV, and gonorrhoea (which requires special tests to distinguish from other *Neisseria* species). Genital and anal warts are the commonest sexually transmitted infections seen in children (Fig. 12.9). Pubic lice can attach to a child's eyelashes rather than head hair; transmission is most often sexual (Fig. 12.10).

Screening for *Neisseria* is recommended:

- For all children who have been sexually abused, especially in cases of penetrative abuse
- For other sexually transmitted infections when one has been found
- If a child <3 years has a sexually transmitted infection, parents should be offered screening to exclude vertical transmission
- For siblings, other adults, and young people within the household
- In consensual sexual contacts in adolescents.

Management of sexual abuse

The management of cases of sexual abuse is hugely involved and may include all of the following.

- Identification of risk
- Multi-agency strategy meeting to plan and coordinate investigation
- Joint investigation including interviews undertaken by police and social worker
- Paediatric forensic examination by trained doctor(s); this may be a joint examination – for example, a paediatrician and a forensic medical examiner
- Identify all children at risk – for example, siblings, friends
- Protect the child – remove the perpetrator if possible
- Identify and support protecting adult(s)
- When risk is considered as ongoing, a protection plan is formulated after a case conference and the child's name placed on the child protection register

- Mental health assessment and treatment – the child may need therapeutic work
- Manage sexually transmitted infections and pregnancy
- Monitor child's safety – provide family support
- Preventive work (child may be at risk of further abuse)
- Therapeutic work for adults involved
- Prosecution is uncommon – around 5% of cases
- Support the professionals – the work is stressful and difficult.

Further reading

Heger A, Emans SJ, Muram D. *Evaluation of the sexually abused child. A medical textbook and photographic atlas.* 2nd ed. Oxford: Oxford University Press, 2001.

Herman-Giddens ME. Vaginal foreign bodies and child sexual abuse. *Arch Pediatric Adolesc Med* 1994;148:195–200.

Hobbs CJ, Hanks HGI, Wynne JM. *Child abuse and neglect. A clinician's handbook.* London: Churchill Livingstone, 1999.

Hobbs CJ, Wynne JM. *Physical signs of child abuse.* 2nd ed. London: W B Saunders, 2001.

Jones DPH, McQuiston MG. *Interviewing the sexually abused child.* 4th ed. London: Gaskell, 1992.

Royal College of Paediatrics and Child Health and the Association of Forensic Physicians *Guidance on paediatric forensic examinations in relation to possible child sexual abuse.* London: RCPCH/AFP, 2004.

Thomas A, Forster G, Robinson A, Rogstad K, for the Clinical Effectiveness Group. National guideline for the management of suspected sexually transmitted infections in children and young people. *Arch Dis Child* 2003;88:303–11.

CHAPTER 13

Child Sexual Abuse: Interpretation of Findings

Donna Rosenberg, Jacqueline Mok

Careful examination of children alleged to have been sexually abused, and the detailed analysis of findings, are relatively recent medical developments. During the past 25 years, techniques and interpretation of findings have changed. Interpretation is based on the best understanding at the time; it changes with increased knowledge.

In the UK the much used guidelines published in the Royal College of Physicians' booklet *Physical signs of sexual abuse in children* classify signs as "diagnostic" or "supportive" of abuse. Currently the Royal College of Paediatrics and Child Health are revising the guidelines, and the degree of specificity attributed to individual signs is yet to be established. The aim will be to maximise both true negative

Table 13.1 Interpretation of physical findings

Finding	Interpretation
Pregnancy	Indicates sexual abuse in a young child
Sperm on specimens taken directly from child's body	Indicates sexual abuse in a young child
Extensive fresh genital/anal trauma; bruising, laceration, bleeding, swelling, bite marks	Indicates abuse if a plausible history is absent
Localised fresh bleeding/ tearing/other trauma to hymen/introitus	Strongly indicates sexual abuse if injury to more external parts of the genitals is absent
Localised fresh trauma to external genitals (labia, pubis, posterior fourchette)	Plausible explanation would include accidental events, especially straddle injuries, which are more likely to result in trauma to external structure, with absence of trauma to more recessed structures (introitus, hymen, intravaginal). If there is no plausible history, sexual abuse is more likely
Absence of hymenal tissue – partial or generalised – with no fresh injury	Depending on the age of the child, sexual abuse is a strong consideration. The relevance of an inferior hymenal cleft is not established
Gaping vaginal opening	May be caused by sexual abuse, but is fairly common in non-abused children. No diameter is known to specifically differentiate. More worrisome in a prepubertal child, especially if the hymen is absent or deeply cleft. Certain conditions may cause the vaginal opening to gape: knee-chest position, deep inspiration, sedation, large/overweight child
Erythema	Non-specific finding. Interpretation is more specific when it is present with other more specific findings. Sometimes difficult to distinguish normal colour from erythema
Vaginal discharge	Common causes include normal discharge, especially in adolescents; non-specific vulvovaginitis; infection unrelated to sexually transmitted infection; sexually transmitted infection
Scars	Infrequent. Do not confuse with normal structures – for example, median raphe. When present on posterior fourchette or hymen, evaluate child for sexual abuse
Labial fusion	Common in girls not sexually abused. Interpretation depends on history and presence of other findings
Bleeding without laceration	Various conditions. Diagnosis depends on site/characteristics/history. Could include urethral prolapse, lichen sclerosus, vaginal/ perianal streptococcus, seborrhoea/eczema, sexual abuse, and others
Perianal swelling, erythema, friability, tenderness, prolapse	Possibilities include sexual abuse, perianal streptococcal infection (no prolapse), inflammatory bowel disease, and others
Perianal venous pooling	Common in children not sexually abused. Interpretation depends on history and presence of other findings

and true positive diagnoses. The information in this chapter reflects the common current guidance (Table 13.1).

Few signs are, in isolation, diagnostic of sexual abuse. Pregnancy or sperm in an 11 year old girl, or in an adolescent with learning difficulty, is the result of abuse because the child could not have given informed consent, whereas pregnancy in a normal adolescent may follow consensual, though not necessarily legal, sex.

In all children extensive genital or anal trauma, or both, with lacerations, bruising, or bite marks strongly indicate sexual assault, unless there is a credible story of accidental injury. Self mutilation is rare. Mutilation incurred during assault is also rare but abused children may give a false account of self injury.

Accidental injuries to the genitals in girls tend to involve external structures – the pubis, labia, perineum, and posterior fourchette – and to spare more recessed structures – such as the hymen and intravaginal walls. Unless there is a clear story of a recent incident, fresh hymenal injuries should lead to immediate investigation for recent child sexual abuse.

Pathological conditions include anal fissures, labial adhesions, friability of the posterior fourchette, and various infections that cause erythema and excoriation – notably, group A streptococcus. Lichen sclerosus et atrophicus presents as thinning and friability of the external genitals in girls (Table 13.2).

Variants of normal anatomy should be distinguished from findings that suggest sexual abuse (Table 13.3). Hyperpigmentation of the labia or perineum is a normal variant, as are perianal or hymeneal tags or bumps. The median raphe is seen as a thin hypopigmented

Table 13.2 Interpretation of infections

Infection	Interpretation
Chlamydia	Can indicate intrapartum or sexual transmission. After about three years, intrapartum transmission cannot be responsible for new onset infection
Gardnerella	Non-specific
Gonorrhoea	Vaginal, pharyngeal, anal: indicates sexual abuse in a young child. Exclude false positives with non-gonorrhoeal *Neisseria* species
Herpes	Sexual abuse should be considered. Genital lesions are unlikely to result from intrapartum transmission or fomites
HIV	Sexual abuse is a strong consideration if mother to child transmission and transmission through blood and blood products can be excluded
Human papillomavirus	Sexual abuse should be considered. Also, consider intrapartum transmission in child aged <18 months. Exclude horizontal transmission
Mixed flora	Non-specific
Molluscum	Unknown to be related to sexual abuse. Laboratory verification needed because it looks similar to herpes or condylomata acuminata
Streptococcus	Unlikely to be related to sexual abuse
Syphilis	Indicates sexual abuse in a young child when vertical transmission and false positive screening test have been excluded

Table 13.3 Normal findings common in children

Girls	Girls and boys
• Periurethral bands • Longitudinal intravaginal ridges • Hymenal tags (in newborns) • Hymenal bumps/mounds • Septate hymen • Smooth notch in superior hymenal rim • Hyperpigmented labia	• Midline avascular perianal line (median raphe) • Perianal skin tags • Smooth perianal areas • Diastasis ani • Perianal hyperpigmentation

line extending down the perineum. Periurethral bands may be seen, as well as many types of hymen, including septate and imperforate. Common perianal variants include skin tags, flattened anal folds, and diastasis ani (smooth areas).

Examination technique

Ideally, the genital or anal examination is done with the use of a colposcope because it provides magnification and can be used for photographic documentation (Fig. 13.1).

The examination of girls is first done with the child supine. Lateral traction of the labia (labial separation) gives a wider field of view to the examiner of the structures recessed between the labia. The vaginal opening may appear smaller with this technique than with gentle outward and slightly downward traction of the labia (labial traction), which tends to make the inferior portion of the introitus more visible. Because outward folding of the posterior hymen may appear similar to an attenuated hymen, irrigation of the region or defining the anatomy with a cotton bud can be used to distinguish the two conditions. Examination in the knee-chest position will show the structures clearly, but some children find this position uncomfortable and embarrassing. The vaginal opening often appears larger than when the child was supine. Anal examination may be done with the child in the supine knee-chest or the left lateral position.

Examination of boys requires no special techniques different than those used during routine examinations.

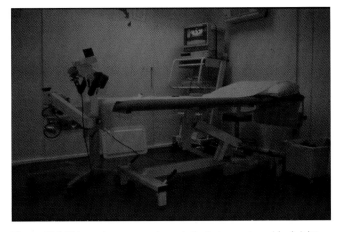

Figure 13.1 Video colposcopy equipment: the instrument provides bright light, magnification, and photographic capability to help in the examination of genitals and anus.

Further reading

Adams JA. Approach to the interpretation of medical and laboratory findings in suspected child abuse: a 2005 revision. *The APSAC Advisor*, Summer 2005: 7–13.

Heger A, Ticson L, Velasquez O, Bernier R. Children referred for possible sexual abuse: medical findings in 2384 children. *Child Abuse Negl* 2002;26:645–59.

Myhre AK, Berntzen K, Bratlid D. Genital anatomy in non-abused preschool girls. *Acta Paediatr* 2003;92:1453–62.

Royal College of Physicians. *The physical signs of sexual abuse in children* London: RCP, 1996. (A new edition by the Royal College of Paediatrics and Child Health is due in 2007)

CHAPTER 14

Non-organic Failure to Thrive

Donna Rosenberg

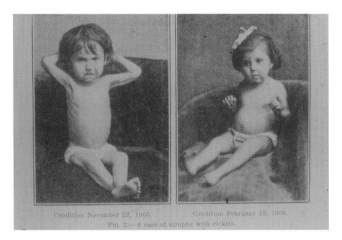

Figure 14.1 A hundred years ago, a plea was made that orphaned institutionalised children with "nutritional atrophy" should be placed in foster homes with an attentive carer. Paired photographs show children with non-organic failure to thrive, before and after foster care.

Non-organic failure to thrive is the condition of the child who is underweight as a result of nutritional deprivation, which is itself the result of emotional deprivation by the parent (Fig. 14.1). The child with non-organic failure to thrive has no medical condition that can account adequately for the wasting. There is a strong association with physical abuse and neglect.

Apart from non-organic failure to thrive, there are two general causes of malnourishment in children: an error in feeding unrelated to deprivation or organic illness. Of all children who present with undernutrition, these causes are more common than nutritional or emotional deprivation.

A feeding error usually involves misunderstanding by, and sometimes poverty of, the parent, but it is unassociated with emotional deprivation. Typical examples are the parent who did not understand (possibly because it was not explained) that clear liquids for the infant's diarrhoea are a temporary treatment, or the poor parent who dilutes the formula to make it last longer. The former sort of parent readily discusses the feeding history, the latter may give an incorrect story because of shame.

Numerous illnesses are associated with failure to thrive; most are detectable by the combination of a thorough history and physical examination and the results of the initial laboratory studies. Abnormalities of any organ system may cause failure to thrive, as

may metabolic, genetic, infectious, immunological, or syndromal anomalies.

Failure to thrive should not be confused with "physiological down regulation." Some babies are born with a weight centile that is higher than that which constitutionally they are destined to achieve. The evolution to a leaner child, with a weight centile lower than that of length or head circumference, may begin gradually between 3 months and 2 years of age, the child appears slender but adequately nourished, has normal developmental milestones, and there is no sign of deprivational behaviour by the carer.

Failure to thrive should also not be confused with short stature. While the weight centile of the child may be lower than that expected from birth weight or age, the weight for height ratio is normal and, most importantly, the child appears healthy and not malnourished though small. The commonest reason for a child being short is having short parents. The child's height centile should be compared with those of the parents.

Diagnosis

The history and physical examination are the critically important tools for diagnosis. If this is done assiduously, many laboratory and other investigations are unnecessary.

Table 14.1 Growth in childhood

Age	Nutritional needs and weight
Birth to 6 months	110 cal/kg/day (0.46 MJ/kg/day) as breast milk or approved infant formula Newborns: about 150 ml/kg milk/day Double birth weight by 4–6 months
6 months to 1 year	105 cal/kg/day (0.44 MJ/kg/day) 6 months: introduction of solids (mushy foods) – families vary widely in their practices, and this is often done earlier than 6 months, mostly without ill effect 10 months: introduction of food that the child can feed itself Type of milk until 1 year: breast milk or approved infant formula Aim to triple birth weight by 1 year
1–3 years	100 cal/kg/day (0.42 MJ/kg/day) Weight gain about 2 kg/year
4–6 years	85–90 cal/kg/day (0.36–0.38 MJ/kg/day) Weight gain about 2 kg/year Average 5 year old weighs about 20 kg
7–10 years	80–85 cal/kg/day (0.33–0.36 MJ/kg/day)

History

A careful history of feeding includes the type and volume of feeds taken and the frequency of feeds. Who decides when the child is to be fed? On what basis? How does the carer know if the child is hungry? Who feeds the child? Is the child fed during the night? In what position is the child fed? Where? Is the bottle sometimes propped? Are water or juice bottles, or both, also given? How often? How much? What is the child's behaviour before and after a feed? While the history is taken, pay close attention to how the parent responds to the child in the examining room.

Infant formula is generally available in three different preparations: ready to feed, liquid concentrate (mix 1:1 with water), and as a powder. If powdered formula is being used, ask how it is mixed and by whom. Also ask how long the tin lasts. If we know the total volume of reconstituted formula that a tin of powder gives and the reported volume and frequency of feeds, we can determine if the tin is lasting much longer than it should if the feeding history was accurate.

At some time before the examination is concluded, the caregiver should be asked to show you how the formula is prepared and to feed the baby.

If the child is breastfed (unusual but not unknown in non-organic failure to thrive), ask in an open ended way about the mother's experience. "Tell me how breastfeeding is going." Establish whether mother reports those symptoms generally indicative of an adequate milk supply – that is, engorgement (fullness/tightening of the breasts before feeding) and breast softness after feeding. Has the mother adamantly opposed supplementation with formula?

A full medical history, review of systems, family history, and social history must be taken, with emphasis on details of the pregnancy, delivery, and postpartum period; immunisations and well baby care; gastrointestinal symptoms; any previous children with failure

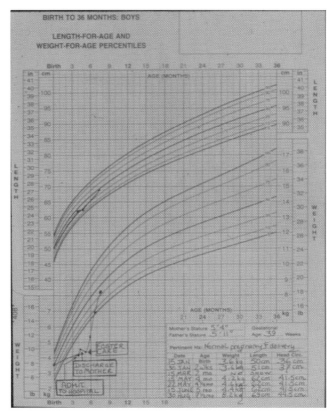

Figure 14.2 Schematic growth chart, showing weights (lower chart) and lengths. Birth weight was at 50th centile but fell below the 5th centile by 4 months. Weight gain was rapid during a brief hospital admission, and dropped again when the child was discharged to the parent. After placement in foster care, weight gain rapidly returned to the expected centile. The length (upper chart) and head circumference (not shown) of this child were not affected. (The recommended growth chart in the UK is the UK90.)

to thrive, illnesses, or who died; paternity of the various children; the living and childcare arrangements, and carer's use of alcohol and drugs.

Usually, a history of feeding well, even ideally, is given for a child with non-organic failure to thrive, but the history is false. The true story of the child having been given inadequate nutrition is concealed. When the child is admitted to hospital or alternative care and given feeds in the volume claimed, the child eats voraciously and gains weight rapidly.

All weights from birth should be gathered and plotted on a standardised growth curve, noting associated centiles, together with all measurements of length and head circumference (Fig. 14.2). (A diligent effort should be made to do the same for each sibling.) While past records are being consulted, check the results of the newborn metabolic screen.

Physical examination

Children with non-organic failure to thrive may be mildly to severely underweight. All have decreased subcutaneous fat stores, and in severely affected children the skin hangs slackly over the underlying tissues (Fig. 14.3). The face, arms, legs, and buttocks usually are affected first by the malnutrition, so that the abdomen gives the

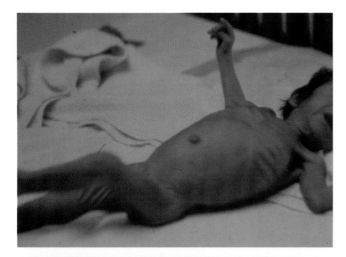

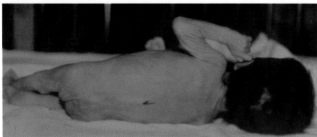

Figure 14.3 This baby with severe failure to thrive was taken to hospital after an anonymous report to social services precipitated a home visit. The parent was an alcoholic, did not go to hospital, had no telephone, and never directly gave a history. Physical examination showed a distressed, emaciated infant with skin hanging slackly from the arms, legs, and buttocks; and nappy rash with considerable skin breakdown. Laboratory studies showed evidence of dehydration and iron deficiency anaemia. Weight gain in hospital was rapid. The infant was discharged to foster care and continued to grow well.

appearance of being distended. In the mildly to moderately affected child, body length and head circumference are normal or near normal; they may also be compromised in severely affected children. Neurological examination often shows hypotonia; much less often the infant is hypertonic. These changes in muscle tone are the consequence, not the cause, of the non-organic failure to thrive and resolve with improved nutrition.

Developmental delay is common, especially in the gross motor domain, and sometimes in the domains of language and personal-social development.

Triceps skinfold thickness, an indicator of total body fat stores, and mid-upper arm circumference, an indicator of total body protein stores, are useful to measure, chart, and follow with time. Typically, both are reduced in non-organic failure to thrive and normalise within a few months of proper nutrition.

A history that gives no indication of an underlying illness, combined with a physical examination that shows no evidence of organic disease are, together, the strongest indicators of non-organic failure to thrive. If this is the case, only a small panel of tests is indicated: full blood count and differential; blood urea, electrolytes, and creatinine concentrations; liver function and thyroid function tests; total protein and albumin concentrations; urinalysis and culture; and bone age study. The purpose of these tests is to establish base-

line laboratory levels of nutritional status and to look for electrolyte, haematological and renal abnormalities that may not be apparent by history and physical examination and that may indicate an organic problem. In mild to moderate non-organic failure to thrive, the results of these tests usually are normal, except that iron deficiency anaemia and delayed bone maturation may be seen. Children with severe failure to thrive may also have hypoproteinaemia, laboratory evidence of dehydration, and electrolyte disturbances. A skeletal survey and toxicology screen should be done, looking for evidence of past physical abuse or drug administration (babies are sometimes given drugs to keep them quiet). The need for other tests depends on the history, physical examination, and initial investigations.

Risks

The mortality associated with non-organic failure to thrive has been reported as 3–12%, but only a small proportion of the deaths are attributable to starvation. Most deaths are the result of physical abuse

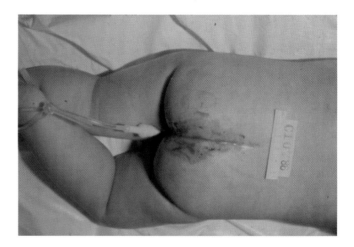

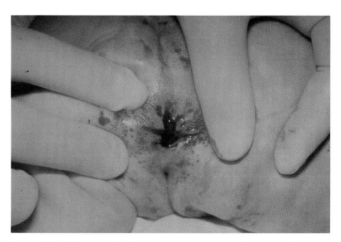

Figure 14.4 This 6 month old presented dead on arrival to hospital. The baby had been returned recently to the care of the mother after a voluntary placement in foster care for moderate non-organic failure to thrive. Physical examination showed a well nourished infant with multiple anal lacerations. There was no laboratory evidence of rape. Postmortem examination showed large, acute subdural haematomas, evidence of intra-abdominal trauma, and anal lacerations that extended 3–4 cm into the rectum. The mother admitted physical abuse.

and, especially in toddlers, supervision neglect, both of which are associated with either current or past non-organic failure to thrive (Fig. 14.4).

Intervention

Most non-organic failure to thrive is seen in infants and represents a crisis. Even when the underweight condition is not itself life threatening, the underlying condition of emotional deprivation by the caregiver is severe, so that the most basic responsibility – that of feeding – has been abandoned for long enough to produce clinical signs in the child. The inadequate emotional attunement and protectiveness of the carer, which may otherwise be hidden, is manifest in the underweight condition of the child.

Acute intervention addresses medical care and placement decisions. Infants who are moderately to severely malnourished should be admitted to hospital for feeding and monitoring, with intake and rate of weight gain documented. Photographs taken on admission are helpful because they make graphic the evidence of measurements that the court may hear. Whether placement out of the home is indicated depends on various factors.

The infant in alternative care should gain weight and thrive, but this does not mean that it is safe to return the child home. There is no standard treatment for the parent of an infant with non-organic failure to thrive; most programmes try to help parents develop appropriate responsiveness to the infant. Sometimes, reasonable success is achieved; sometimes, the parent's apathy, disinterest, and lack of attachment do not change.

Box 14.1 Suggested criteria for immediate placement out of home in cases of non-organic failure to thrive

- Infant is seriously malnourished
- Evidence of physical abuse of child
- Parent will not participate in treatment programme (willingness may be expressed but is contradicted by lack of action)
- Parent is psychotic
- Past attempts at home placement have failed
- Events/history of siblings indicate that staying at home is unlikely to be safe

---

Further reading

Frank DA, Drotar D, Cook JT, Bleiker JS, Kasper D. Failure to thrive. In: *Child abuse and neglect: medical diagnosis and management*. 2nd ed. Reece RM, Ludwig S, eds. Philadelphia, PA: Lippincott Williams & Wilkins, 2001:307–38.

Oates RK, Kempe RS. Growth failure in infants. In: *The battered child*. 5th ed. Helfer ME, Kempe RS, Krugman RD, eds. Chicago: University of Chicago Press, 1997:374–91.

CHAPTER 15

Neglect

Donna Rosenberg, Hendrika Cantwell

Parents have rights regarding their children. They also have duties to those children (Table 15.1). Child neglect is the failure to perform these duties.

The concept of parental duty appears in the law and is based on the combination of a biological truth and a social imperative. The biological truth is that the rate at which human offspring develop the skills for independence is slow compared with that of most other mammals. Children take years before they are able to gather food, protect themselves from the elements or predators, recognise and handle danger, or are capably socialised. During these years, they rely on adults of the species for survival, protection, and teaching (Fig. 15.1). The social imperative is that parents, not society or the state, are responsible for children. The state does not wish to intrude on or usurp either the rights or the responsibilities of parents. The aphorism "it takes a village to raise a child" is not represented in the law. The law provides only that, when parents seriously fail in their duty, the "village" is obliged to intervene on behalf of the dependent child.

The standard to which parents are held in the performance of their duty cannot be a standard of perfect care. No parent is capable of that, and the law neither defines nor requires it. Generally, the standard of care to which parents are held is that of the reasonable

Table 15.1 Purpose of parental duties

Duty	Purpose
Food	Growth and development
Clothing	Protect the child adequately
Shelter	Protect the child from extreme weather, keep them safe, and allow a place for sleep
Safekeeping	Prevent reasonably foreseeable and avoidable injury or illness
Nurturance	Promote attachment on which development of empathy and other characteristics largely depend
Teaching	Move the child towards being independent in a way that is safe for the child and not dangerous to others

or prudent parent. Assessing that standard depends on the cultural context. Though it is vital that the cultural background and practices of the family be understood and respected, they must not over-rule a child's basic rights.

From a practical point of view, parental duties are those that are central to a child's survival and development and that serve a defined purpose. In most families, parents are driven to meet their

Figure 15.1 Humans and chimpanzees require many years to achieve maturity. Most other mammals do so more quickly. (Mother and baby reproduced with permission from Mary Motley Kalergis.)

responsibilities not because they are legally bound but because they love the child.

The types of neglect that are more likely to be seen in a medical setting are discussed here, but there are others, such as neglect of education.

Medical care neglect

Medical care is a form of safekeeping (Box 15.1). In regard to medical care, when a parent's imprudent and avoidable acts of omission or commission result in substantial temporary or permanent harm, considerable risk of such harm, or the death of a child, the child is medically neglected (Box 15.2).

Parental neglect can range from mild to severe, as can the consequences to the child, but these are not always proportional. For example, sometimes the neglect is mild but the child's outcome severe.

Regular visits for medical care are especially necessary in infancy and toddlerhood. Early diagnosis and secondary prevention of particular conditions is the main purpose. A history and physical examination are the chief tools for detecting congenital hip dysplasia, neurological problems, growth abnormalities, developmental delays, strabismus, tumours, and undernutrition. Immunisations, also needed, are a form of primary prevention.

Some children are medically neglected in the context of a new and acute event, others in the context of a chronic medical condition – for example, asthma, diabetes, renal failure, cancer, or a congenital syndrome. In the chronically ill child, the parent has the duty to seek continuing medical care for the child only when the benefits of such care exceed the risks.

As children get older, depending on their intellectual and motor skills, they may be able to assume greater responsibility. While they are minors the final responsibility is the parents'. This can be a trying situation for the parents of, for example, a rebellious adolescent girl with diabetes.

There are many reasons why parents fail to seek medical care, including misunderstanding; lack of judgment – for example, underestimation of the severity of the problem; lack of motivation; exhaustion, especially in parents of chronically ill children; cost; religious beliefs; fear – for example, of the diagnosis, or of being criticised for poor care; illness; limited intellect; transport or other logistical problem; unhappiness with previous medical care. Whether identification of neglect is sound depends on a combination of the reason for the failure to seek medical care and the context in which it occurred (Box 15.3).

Box 15.1 **Parental duties of medical care**

- Make a reasonable attempt to prevent illness, including injury
- Recognise obviously severe illness in the child
- Bring, or diligently try to bring, the seriously ill child for medical care without delay
- Comply, or diligently try to comply, with medical instruction that, if carried out, would be more likely than not to reduce or eliminate the considerable risk of substantial harm

---

Box 15.2 **Physical evidence of medical care neglect**

Document:
- Severe symptoms and signs
- Subtherapeutic concentrations of prescribed drugs
- Metabolic/other abnormalities – acute
- Metabolic/other abnormalities – chronic

Few circumstances will yield positive results in all four categories, but many will yield positives in at least one

Example:
A 5 year old girl with renal failure requires home dialysis and many drugs. Her long term outlook is reasonable; she is on the waiting list for a transplant. In the past, her parents' compliance has been unreliable. Now, she presents to hospital in a coma after not receiving dialysis for four days.
- Symptoms and signs: drowsy, vomiting, hypertensive
- Drug concentrations: none subtherapeutic
- Acute metabolic abnormalities: serum potassium and creatinine concentrations greatly raised, acidosis
- Chronic metabolic changes: unexceptional

Supervision neglect

Supervision is a form of safekeeping. Parents have a duty to protect the child from situations and people they know, or should have known, to be dangerous, and the duty to intervene on behalf of the child in a timely way. Supervision neglect occurs when the parent fails to provide attendance, guidance, and protection to a child who cannot comprehend or anticipate danger.

Parents are expected to carry out this duty within the boundaries of their capabilities, assuming those capabilities have not been compromised by the parents themselves. For example, a drunken parent, but not a parent restricted to a wheelchair, may be accountable for failure to rescue a child in a fire.

Supervision neglect occurs either when:
- The parent is in the home or with the child but does not attend to the child; the parent may or may not be impaired by drugs, alcohol, illness, immaturity, or low intelligence, *or*
- The parent is not in the home or with the child, and has entrusted the child either to a babysitter or a sibling who is not capable of providing adequate supervision.

Box 15.3 **Was there medical care neglect?**

- What were the potential benefits of medical care?
- What were the potential risks of medical care?
- What was the expected outcome in the child without medical care? Did the parents know this?
- Did the parents have access to medical care?
- Did the parents have access to transport?
- What was the parents' record in getting medical care for the child?
- To what extent did the failure to seek appropriate medical care influence outcome?
- Was the parents' conduct acceptable within their own culture? Is the cultural standard less than reasonable?

Figure 15.2 Carers are responsible for ensuring that children do not have access to harmful substances.

Most parents try to protect their children from harm in a manner that is relevant to the child's age and developmental stage, realising that each age is associated with behaviours that may prove hazardous unless supervised or stopped. Though none of the following examples in isolation constitutes supervision neglect, each of the circumstances is commonly associated with parental failure to supervise the child:

- Fire
- Falls from windows and down stairs
- Drowning
- Poisoning and ingestion of toxic substances or dangerous objects (Fig. 15.2)
- Leaving children unattended in cars, resulting in hypothermia, hyperthermia, or dehydration.
- Road traffic incidents as a result of leaving children unattended.

Though some children who are a little less than 12 years old can be alone safely for short periods, the danger lies in the assumption that they can be alone or minding younger siblings every day for extended periods, without a responsible adult nearby. Early adolescent boys are more likely to abuse drugs if they are home alone two hours

Table 15.2 What is needed to supervise?

• Attention span	• Mental state not impaired
• Enough experience from which to generalise	• Memory
• Ability to defer own needs	• Ability to recognise an emergency and carry out instructions

Box 15.4 **Constellation of findings suggests supervision neglect**

The police brought a child to the paediatric clinic. Physical examination showed an infected digit with embedded sutures (Fig. 15.3a), a 2 cm semicircular mark near the mouth (Fig. 15.3b), an old unilateral V shaped burn on the lateral chest (Fig. 15.3c), and a moderately severe nappy rash.

Apparently weeks previously the child had his finger accidentally trapped in a car door. The top of the finger had been partly severed and he had been treated at another hospital. The mother failed to attend follow-up appointments. He had pulled a hot drink on to himself recently; no medical care had been sought. The nappy rash had been there for a long time. The cause of the perioral mark was unknown (perhaps having resulted from the child chewing an electrical cord).

a day after school or ten hours a week. Moreover, adults who prey on children will befriend those whom they see always alone.

An important aspect of premature "self care" (sometimes a euphemism for supervision neglect) is that the child assumes himself to be competent. As the child grows older, he rejects parental restrictions. From a 14 year old's point of view, it makes sense to challenge parental limits, such as "You can't stay out all night," when he was caring for himself at the age of 8.

Whether an injury to a child was the result of an "accident" or occurred in the context of "supervision neglect" is not a distinction

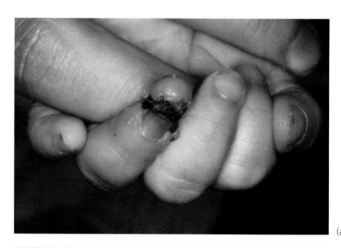

(a)

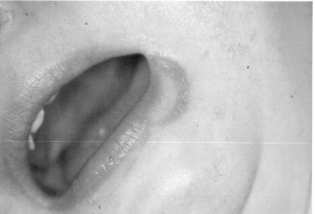

(b)

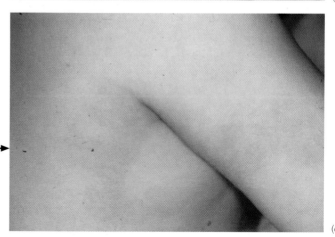

(c)

Figure 15.3 Infected finger (a), semicircular mark near mouth (b), V shaped burn on lateral chest (c).

that lends itself to tidy analysis (Table 15.3). On the one hand, the parent is perpetually on a learning curve and, sometimes, learns what is prudent only after the fact. On the other hand, some injuries are characterised by features that are both unusual and tend to offend the reasonable standard: repetitive injuries to the child despite cognitive understanding by the parent or extreme failure to safeguard the child, or both.

Developmental neglect

In the best circumstances, children have both developmental support and the opportunity to make use of natural attributes. At the other extreme is developmental neglect, which involves lack of stimulation of the child, restriction or forbidding of natural developmental impetus, lack of teaching, and lack of reasonably consistent limit setting. Severe neglect may result in delayed developmental milestones or aberrant behaviour. In the developmentally delayed child, care must be taken to distinguish neglect from the many other possible causes.

Delayed or aberrant personal-social development may result from lack of stimulation. Sensory stimulation and communicating with an infant begin in infancy, with holding, eye contact, talking, and playing. The neglected infant, left alone most of the time with a propped bottle, is isolated.

Silent infants are worrisome. A search for an organic cause, including hearing impairment, must be undertaken. The hearing of sounds stimulates language development. Language delay secondary to neglect may stunt intellectual development.

Motor delay may result from severe parental restriction, sometimes amounting to incarceration. Gross motor impulses, such as sitting, crawling, walking, running, and jumping, should have an outlet (this is sometimes difficult in cramped housing) with walks and visits to parks and playgrounds.

The setting of limits by adults is a form of teaching and begins early in a child's life. A child starts to assume some responsibility for self control at about 3 or 3 1/2 years. Gradually, by repetitive, non-abusive, and consistent teaching of limits, the child develops the ability to exercise restraint. This is self discipline, an internalisation of "no," – that is, of the capacity to delay or deny impulse. It is absent in the school age child who will not attend or behave in class, assaults other students, is frequently "sent to the head's office," and exhausts the teacher. Children who have experienced neglect in limit setting may have behaviour identical with that of children with attention deficit hyperactivity disorder, and the two conditions must be distinguished. The risk of limit setting neglect is that the

Table 15.3 Accident or supervision neglect?

What was:	
• Child's age	• Parents' physical and mental capabilities
• Developmental stage	
• Period unsupervised	• History of chronic supervision neglect
• Circumstances	• Cultural acceptability (less than reasonable?)
• Potential hazard (how obvious was it/should it have been?)	• Contribution of poverty

Table 15.4 Neglect unlikely to be caused by poverty

• Attachment – poor or absent	• Lack of emotional nurturance or guidance
• Failure to feed adequately, though food available	• Chronic deprecatory remarks to child
• Chronic or flagrant failure to supervise	• Failure to ensure medical care
• Lack of limit setting	• Failure to ensure school attendance
• Lack of developmental stimulation	

child emerges as an adult with poor impulse control. When this is combined with a limited capacity for empathy – an effect of emotional maltreatment – it is a particularly antisocial and sometimes dangerous combination.

Neglect and poverty or wealth

Neglect and poverty sometimes coexist and may be causally or co-incidentally related. It is important to distinguish the neglect that is caused by poverty from the neglect that is not because the interventions are different (Table 15.4). Neglectful behaviour that exists with poverty but is not caused by it is not improved by giving the family money or resources.

Any form of neglect may be found also in middle class and wealthy families. Though nutritional and medical care neglect are rare, limit setting neglect is common. Children from these families tend to come to light at a later age than do the children of poor families and are sometimes first encountered by social services or police when they are apprehended in the context of a criminal act.

Misdiagnosis of neglect

If diagnosis of neglect is possible, so is misdiagnosis (Fig. 15.5).

Table 15.5 Misdiagnosis of child neglect

The following conditions do not constitute evidence of child neglect:

• Untidiness	• Nappy rash
• Lice	• Bald spot/thin hair
• Scabies	• Flat head (brachycephaly)
• Impetigo	• Malnourishment – many forms
• Insect bites	• Dyslexia

Further reading

Dubowitz H, Black MM. Child neglect. In: *Child abuse: medical diagnosis and management*. 2nd ed. Reece RM, Ludwig S, eds. Philadelphia, PA: Lippincott Williams & Wilkins, 2001.

Dubowitz H, ed. *Neglected children*. Thousand Oaks, CA: Sage Publications, 1999.

Polansky NA, Chalmers MA, Buttenwiesser EW, Williams DP. *Damaged parents: an anatomy of child neglect*. Chicago, IL: University of Chicago, 1981.

Rosenberg DA, Cantwell H. The consequences of neglect – individual and societal. In: Hobbs CJ, Wynne JM, eds. *Balliere's clinical paediatrics: international practice and research – child abuse*. Vol 1. London: Balliere Tindall, Harcourt Brace Jovanovich; 1993:185–210.

CHAPTER 16

Emotional Abuse

Danya Glaser

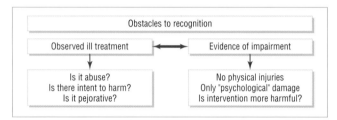

Figure 16.1 Obstacles to recognition

Box 16.1 **Threshold definition for emotional abuse**

- Aspects of a RELATIONSHIP, not a single event or series of events
- Interactions that PERVADE/characterise parent-child relationship
- Actually or potentially HARMFUL to the child
- Includes OMISSION and COMMISSION
- NO PHYSICAL contact with the child is necessary as part of the emotional abuse

There is a widely held belief that emotional abuse is difficult to define and therefore to recognise (Fig. 16.1). In fact, unlike sexual abuse, which is a secret activity, emotional abuse is observable. The perceived difficulty is in naming the observed interactions as emotional abuse. Part of the difficulty lies with the term "abuse," which is often associated with an intention to harm the child. There is professional reluctance to regard harmful parent-child interactions as abuse, and consequent delay and under-recognition of emotional abuse.

From a utilitarian perspective abuse can be regarded as any experience that is actually or potentially harmful to the child and that therefore warrants some kind of intervention. At all times, and especially where there is hesitancy in naming emotional abuse or neglect, simple description is a powerful tool.

Definitions

In *Working Together to Safeguard Children* emotional abuse is defined as follows:

"Emotional abuse is the persistent emotional ill-treatment of a child such as to cause severe and persistent adverse effects on the child's emotional development. It may involve conveying to children that they are worthless or unloved, inadequate, or valued only insofar as they meet the needs of another person. It may feature age or developmentally inappropriate expectations being imposed on children. It may involve causing children frequently to feel frightened or in danger, or the exploitation or corruption of children. Some level of emotional abuse is involved in all types of ill treatment of a child, though it may occur alone."

Emotional neglect is subsumed within the category of neglect:

"Neglect . . . may also include neglect of, or unresponsiveness to a child's basic emotional needs."

Unlike other forms of child abuse, emotional abuse and neglect is not recognised by observing the child. Indicators of impairment in the child may draw attention to the need to explain the child's difficulty, but emotional abuse can be confirmed only by recognising the ill treatment. An alternative way to approach emotional abuse is to define a threshold within which it is possible to describe many different forms of interaction (Box 16.1).

If the parent-child interaction satisfies the definitional criteria, the threshold for emotional abuse or neglect is reached. Pervasiveness is assessed during observation and is evidenced by descriptions that include terms such as "always," "usually," or "often," observed at different times, in different settings, and by different people.

To aid identification and better understand the meaning of the emotional abuse, these various interactions can be conceptually organised within five categories of ill treatment. These five categories are presented with examples.

Categories of ill treatment within emotional abuse and neglect

Emotional unavailability, unresponsiveness, and neglect – The primary carer(s) are usually preoccupied with their own particular difficulties such as mental ill health (including postnatal depression) and substance abuse, or overwhelming work commitments. They

Box 16.2 **Lack of interaction**

- Extremely little or no emotional or psychological interaction between the carer and the child (emotional unavailability)
- The carer fails to respond to the child's overtures or attempts to interact with the carer (unresponsiveness)

Box 16.3 Criticism and rejection

- The child is repeatedly harshly criticised or denigrated by the carer
- The child is treated as a "scapegoat" by the carer
- The child is rejected by the carer

Box 16.4 Unrealistic expectations

- The child is given responsibility that they are developmentally unable to fulfil or that impedes their development – for example, education, peer relationships
- The child is disciplined in an inconsistent, harsh, or inappropriate manner because of the carer's lack of awareness or understanding
- The child is overprotected or his/her exploration limited
- The child is exposed to confusing, distressing, disturbing, or bizarre behaviour – for example, intrafamilial (domestic) violence and parental (para) suicide

are unable or unavailable to respond to the child's emotional needs, with no provision of an adequate alternative (Box 16.2).

Negative attributions to and interactions with the child – The parent or primary caregiver(s) holds beliefs about the child's bad character and attributions, which may have been inherited from a disliked person. The child, who could be singled out in a sibling group, is viewed as deserving a negative stance (Box 16.3).

Developmentally inappropriate or inconsistent interactions with the child – The parents lack knowledge of age appropriate caregiving and disciplining practices and child development, often because of their own childhood experiences. Their interactions with their children, while harmful, are thoughtless and misguided rather than intending harm (Box 16.4).

Failure to recognise or acknowledge the child's individuality and psychological boundary – The parent(s) cannot recognise an appropriate psychological boundary between the parent and the child and is unable to distinguish between the child's reality and the adult's beliefs and wishes (Box 16.5).

Failing to promote the child's social adaptation – The carer fails to consider or recognise the child's needs in social interactions and functioning outside the family (Box 16.6).

Several categories may be found within one parent-child relationship. It is, however, usually clear which one is the "driving" category that underpins the manifestations of emotional abuse of the child.

Effects on the child: impairment of health and development

There are no indicators of harm or impairment of the child's functioning or development that are specific to emotional abuse and

Box 16.5 Using the child

- The child is used by the carer in the carer's conflict with another person
- The child is expected to fulfil the carer's own unfulfilled ambitions
- In fabricated or induced illness, the carer, for his or her own needs, wants the child to be treated as ill

Box 16.6 Mis-socialisation

- The child is allowed or encouraged to be involved in antisocial and criminal activities, including drug misuse (mis-socialisation)
- The child is deprived of the opportunity to develop peer relationships, including isolation of the child
- Failure to provide adequate cognitive stimulation, education and/or experiential learning; intellectual deprivation (psychological neglect)

neglect. Emotional abuse cannot therefore be recognised by the presentation of the child. There are, however, various manifestations of the harm caused to children who are, or have been, emotionally abused (Box 16.7). They are important and an explanation needs to be sought. Chronic difficulties and recurrent unexplained medical problems should draw attention to the possibility of emotional abuse and neglect.

Severity

An assessment of severity must include the actual or likely effect on the child. Factors to be considered include the age of the child at onset (bearing in mind that recognition in later childhood may indicate late recognition rather than late onset); duration of the abuse; the "intensity" of the harmful interaction; protective factors such as the child's innate ability and the availability of a trusted adult; and secure attachment relationships.

Cultural issues

It would seem that the categories of ill treatment are universally applicable, though there is cultural variation in the parent-child interactions – for example, that which is deemed developmentally appropriate. Such issues require sensitive and thoughtful practice, bearing in mind that all children are entitled to the same threshold of protection and that certain apparently cultural practices may not be benign or indeed culturally sanctioned.

Box 16.7 Effect on the child

Emotional state
- Lack of response or extreme response to separation from parents
- Unhappy/depressed/withdrawn
- Self soothing/rocking
- Frightened/distressed
- Very anxious
- Low self esteem

Behaviour
- Attention seeking
- Oppositional/aggressive
- Age-inappropriate responsibility for younger children or for parent
- Antisocial/delinquent

Peer relationships
- Isolated
- Aggressive

Developmental/educational attainment
- Developmental delay
- Educational underachievement
- Non-attendance at school or persistent lateness

Physical state
- Small stature or poor growth
- Physically neglected or unkempt
- Unexplained pains
- Very disturbed sleep
- Encopresis without constipation

Though the third stage is less common than the other two, it features more prominently in child care and criminal proceedings because of the strength of the evidence, which may include detailed toxicology reports, video recordings, and other robust forensic evidence.

Box 17.1 Severe abuse resulting from false illness story

A boy had nine colonoscopies, a bronchoscopy, gastroscopy, two jejunal biopsies, and angiography. He incurred a Nissen fundoplication and an ileostomy and lived on total parenteral nutrition for four years. The mother did not harm him directly; she merely presented a false story about his intractable vomiting and diarrhoea. After separation from his mother the child fed normally and became healthy.

Clinical features

Young preschool children are the main victims. The abuse usually starts in the first year of life, often within the first month (and sometimes even earlier – unusual events in pregnancy are common). It is uncommon after the age of 5 and then sometimes involves a degree of awareness or complicity by the older child for the false illness to continue to deceive doctors. Boys and girls are equally affected.

Epidemiology

The two year survey of fabricated or induced illness in the UK, using British Paediatric Surveillance unit ascertainment, suggested that the annual incidence for children under the age of 1 is about 3 per 100 000. Nearly half the siblings of index children experience either similar or another form of abuse. There is an increased incidence of unexpected death in previous children

Presentation

The child usually presents with problems relating to one system – for instance, recurrent seizures or a story of diarrhoea and vomiting (Tables 17.1 and 17.2). A minority present as if they have a multisystem disorder. Some of the children will have genuine illness in addition to the superimposed illness – thus a child may have occasional genuine seizures but be presented as having many seizures each day. A wide range of physical signs is fabricated.

Table 17.1 Presentations

Common presentations	
Nervous system	Seizures, drowsiness, ataxia
Gastrointestinal	Vomiting, diarrhoea, failure to thrive
Respiratory	Apnoea, breathlessness, haemoptysis
Renal	Haematuria, biochemical abnormality
Endocrine/metabolic	Glycosuria, biochemical abnormality
Unusual allergy	Rashes, diarrhoea, vomiting, swelling
Less common presentations	
Ear/nose/throat	Bleeding, discharge, foreign bodies
Skin	Abscesses, dermatitis artefacta
Orthopaedic	Locked joints, arthritis
Haematological	Anaemia, bleeding
Immune system	Fevers, infections
Cardiovascular	Arrhythmias, pallor/cyanosis
Educational	Dyslexia, disability, special needs

Table 17.2 Factitious signs

Signs	Cause
Bleeding	Haematemesis, haemoptysis, haematuria, or other bleeding. Usually the mother uses her own blood
Seizures	Hypoxia (smothering), drugs, salt
Failure to thrive	Withholding or diluting food, sucking back feed from stomach with a nasogastric tube
Diarrhoea	Laxatives
Vomiting	Emetics, fingers pushed down child's throat, or mother presents own vomit as child's
Fevers	Falsifying chart or heating thermometer. Contamination of intravenous line with saliva, faeces, or dirty water
Dermatitis	Caustic solutions, scratching or injuring the skin (Fig. 17.2)
Chronic discharge	From ears, vagina, anus, by repetitive poking with small object
Anaemia	By venepuncture or disconnecting IV line to drain blood
Metabolic	Addition of drug or chemical to child's urine or blood sample

Usually the story of illness is presented consistently by the mother and the periodic events of illness start only in her presence. The father may be unusually absent from visits to outpatient clinics or the ward. While some mothers are model parents in terms of keeping appointments and complying with treatment, it is quite common to find a paradoxical mixture of pleading for more treatment and investigation on the one hand and failure to attend for such tests and appointments on the other (presumably because the mother knows they are not needed). Compliance with treatment may be chaotic: though apnoea alarms are issued they are not used appropriately, and prescribed anticonvulsants are not given for a period and then given in excess. Unusual failure of equipment is common, with lines becoming disconnected or infected and catheters breaking.

The mothers usually stay with one general practitioner and, when referred to hospital, with one specialist. The child's referral to other specialists is made by the general practitioner or specialist, and the child may be transferred from one centre of excellence to another; repetitive investigation results.

Consequences

The consequences of fabricated or induced illness are repetitive, unpleasant, or dangerous investigations and treatments. Induced illness as a result of the mother's actions (for example, from injection of contaminated solutions into intravenous lines) can lead to disability or death. Chronic invalidism can occur as a result of the child being indoctrinated with the concept of being ill. Abnormal illness behaviour when the child grows up (sometimes amounting to Munchausen's syndrome) can be a result of being encouraged and taught to participate in the deception of doctors; this is a serious but less common outcome.

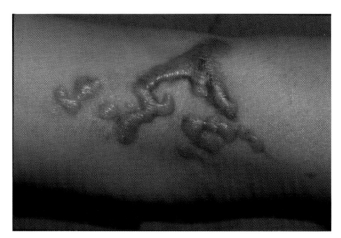

Figure 17.2 Keloid scars on the arm resulting from repetitive application of caustic sodium hydroxide. For over a year the dermatitis artefacta, involving different parts of the body, was thought to be a rare natural skin disorder.

Box 17.2 **Warning signals***

Illness
- Unexplained, recurrent, and persistent
- Very rare

Symptoms and signs
- Incongruous
- Only when mother present
- Unusual allergy

Mother
- Hospital addict
- Not too worried
- Publicity seeking

Father
- Uninvolved with child's "illness"

Treatment
- Ineffective
- Not tolerated

Family
- Previous unexplained child death
- Child abuse
- Multiple illness

Pets
- Sudden death
- Unusual illnesses

*No signal individually has high specificity or sensitivity

Perpetrator

In over 90% of cases the perpetrator is the child's natural mother. In 5% of cases it is another female carer, and in less than 5% it is the child's father. It is unusual for there to be collusion between the mother and father; the partner is usually unaware and initially dumbfounded by the allegation.

Commonly, the perpetrating mother has incurred emotional abuse as a child, particularly lack of love and respect from her own mother. Women with a nursing background are over-represented among perpetrators. Previous encounters with a psychiatrist are common, but it is rare for the mother to have an identified mental illness. Most of them have personality disorders; about half have somatising disorders. Male perpetrators are similar, though histrionic personality characteristics and Munchausen's syndrome itself are more common in men.

Some of the mothers are hospital addicts, who seem to relish a good paediatric unit. They form close relationships with the staff and take the lead in fund raising. Other perpetrators, however, behave more like the usual parents who abuse children, being reluctant to visit their child in hospital, and being over-ready to complain or be litigious about medical care.

Many mothers achieve considerable self respect from their role in caring for an "ill" child and cherish their close relationship with doctors, nurses, and support agencies, while others gain sympathy within their family and their communities (as a result of seeking publicity), as well as support from parents of other sick children. For some the motive seems to be to reclaim an absent husband. There are some cases, however, in which resentment and violence feature high in the motivation – the mother resenting the impact of the baby on her life or being unable to tolerate the problems of caring for a child.

Warning signals

General features are listed in Box 17.2. Clinics providing certain highly specialised services for children are more likely to encounter factitious illness; these include clinics providing intensive treatment for intractable epilepsy, severe allergy, recurrent apnoea, or sleep apnoea; those supervising prolonged parenteral feeding; and those assessing children for Nissen fundoplication because of seemingly severe gastro-oesophageal reflux.

Action and reaction

Extreme fabricated illness is serious and may be life threatening, requiring immediate liaison with social services and the police to protect the child. It is important not to over-react, however, just because a mother is lying or fabricating signs. Sometimes a mother may add blood to her child's urine or alter a temperature chart to dissuade the doctors from discharging the child from hospital before the mother is sufficiently reassured and ready to cope at home. Such minor events should be sorted out sympathetically and promptly in a way that dissuades the mother from giving false illness stories or fabricating signs again. More commonly, mothers perceive or exaggerate their child's symptoms because of anxiety and stress.

Usually the diagnosis is a paediatric one. An experienced paediatrician is needed to decide whether the child's symptoms and signs are the results of natural illness or are false. Additional opinions will be needed to consider the possibility of rare disorders. In some cases – for instance, fictitious sexual abuse or imposed psychological symptoms – a child psychiatrist or child psychologist may be the most appropriate expert.

Establishing that the illness is factitious can be difficult and requires much resourcefulness (Box 17.3). Verification of the alleged

---

Box 17.3 **Diagnostic strategy**

- Review all records
  - Index child and siblings
  - GP, hospital, community
- Obtain history from other sources
  - Relatives, nursery, teachers
- Consider all natural causes
  - Opinions of paediatric specialists
- Seek evidence of fabrication
  - Toxicology, blood groups, video monitoring
- Consider trial separation

illness events should be sought from other family members. Contact with the general practitioner and health visitor are important, and their records can be checked against the hospital records for consistency of illness events (Box 17.4). Every opportunity should be taken to acquire forensic evidence by way of toxicological evidence or testing to determine the origin of blood in a sample or on clothing. Trial separation – a period of observation in hospital, or alternative care without visits from the parents, can be a much kinder and more useful diagnostic test for the child than yet more invasive investigations.

Sherlock Holmes to Dr Watson:
"How often have I said to you that when you have eliminated the impossible, whatever remains, however improbable, must be the truth?" *The Sign of Four* (1890)

The long term outcome for children who have been abused by fictitious illness is worrying. There is a considerable incidence of recurrence of abuse of children who remain in maternal care and considerable morbidity in the long term, suggesting that such abuse reflects a serious disorder of the carer-child relationship and the chance of long lasting harm.

Not quite fabricated or induced illness

There are times when severe fabricated or induced illness seems to be an extension of commonplace parental behaviour concerning their child's health, and of discrepancies in patient/doctor expectations and interaction. Each of the types of parental behaviour listed below is well recognised and not rare. Though they may be disadvantageous to the child and sometimes harmful, most of the time the behaviour is contained by appropriate medical help and counselling. In some circumstances, however, each of these behaviour patterns may be a cause of serious child abuse and may necessitate child protection procedures.

Overanxious parents – Some parents communicate their own extreme anxiety to the child, thereby perpetuating and enhancing adverse behaviour or ill health. Some mothers perceive symptoms out of fearfulness or exaggerate them to impress doctors. Impatient doctors compound the problem.

Doctor shopping – For a parent to seek a second or third opinion about their child may be sensible, but an eighth or ninth further opinion is likely to be abusive in terms of repeated investigation and needless treatment.

False allegations of paternal abuse in the context of custody disputes – The usual motive for this is the prevention of one parent having access to the child.

Hysteria by proxy – A mother who believes that she has an unusual allergy or incapacitating postviral syndrome can impose the same symptoms on her child.

Delusional disorder – Mothers who have genuine mental illness can be deluded about their child's incapacity or illness.

Further reading

Bools CN, Neale BA, Meadow SR. Co-mordidity associated with fabricated illness (Munchausen syndrome by proxy). *Arch Dis Child* 1992;67:77–9.

Davis PM, McClure RJ et al. Procedures, placement and risks of further abuse after Munchausen syndrome by proxy, non-accidental poisoning and non-accidental suffocation (BPSU survey). *Arch Dis Child* 1998;78:217–21.

Department of Health. *Safeguarding children in whom illness is induced or fabricated by carers with parental responsibilities*. London: DoH, 2001.

Eminson M, Postlethwaite RJ. *Munchausen syndrome by proxy abuse: a practical approach*. London: Arnold, 2001.

McClure RJ, Davis PM, Meadow SR, Sibert JR. Epidemiology of Munchausen syndrome by proxy, non-accidental poisoning and non-accidental suffocation (BPSU survey). *Arch Dis Child* 1996;**75**:57–61.

Rosenberg DA. Munchausen syndrome by proxy. In: Reece RM, Ludwig S, eds. *Child abuse medical diagnosis and management*. Philadelphia, PA: Lippincott Williams & Wilkins, 2001:363–83.

Royal College of Paediatrics and Child Health. *Fabricated or induced illness by carers*. London: RCPCH, 2002.

CHAPTER 18

Role of the Child and Adolescent Mental Health Team

Fiona Forbes

Table 18.1 Roles of the CAMH team in child protection

- Clinical: assessment and treatment
- Consultation
- Teaching and training
- Policy planning
- Court work
- Audit and research

Child abuse is a non-specific risk factor for psychiatric disorders and mental and physical health problems in childhood, adolescence, and adulthood. The effects of abuse will vary, depending on several factors.

The child and adolescent mental health (CAMH) team is usually a multidisciplinary team that may have members from psychiatry, clinical psychology, nursing, community or primary mental health work, occupational therapy, psychotherapy, and social work. Most will operate as generic teams, but, especially in larger centres, there may be teams specialising in services for abused children.

The main role for the team is in the assessment and treatment of mental health problems linked to abuse. There are, however, other functions of the team (Table 18.1).

Clinical

Promotion of a safe, nurturing environment

- After investigation of child abuse and neglect, a multi-agency approach in the further management of the child and family may be indicated. This needs to be well coordinated, with every professional clear about his or her role.
- It is important that the child is no longer exposed to abuse or neglect. Specific treatment for the child is unlikely to be effective if the child remains unsafe.

Interventions for parents

There is a range of interventions that may help. More than one may be appropriate, either at the same time or sequentially.

The outcome for the child will be improved if there is a non-abusive parent who has support and good coping strategies and who recognises the importance of protecting the child (Table 18.2). Interventions can try to boost these protective factors – for instance, providing support (emotional and practical) and promoting problem solving skills in these parents (Table 18.3).

Some parents may benefit from advice on managing their children's behaviour using the principles of behaviour therapy. Empha-

Table 18.2 Possible adverse outcomes

Type of abuse	Possible adverse outcome
Emotional abuse or neglect: impact is most profound if it is experienced in the first two years of life	• Failure to thrive • Attachment disorders • Concentration and learning • Poor interpersonal relationships • Aggression
Physical abuse	• 30% of abused children grow up to be abusive parents • Attachment disorders • Post-traumatic stress disorder • Externalising behaviour problems (aggression, delinquency) • Poor peer relationships • Academic underachievement
Sexual abuse	• Sexualised behaviours • Self harming behaviours • Post-traumatic stress disorder • Chronic low mood • Depression • Drug and alcohol misuse • Bulimia nervosa
Witnessing domestic violence	• Anxiety and fears • Sleep disturbances • Depression • Aggression • Poor interpersonal relationships

In addition, there is a high incidence of child abuse and neglect in families in which domestic violence is commonplace

sis is on identification, promotion, and reward of good behaviour in the child. Individual and group approaches have been developed. The CAMH team may work with parents directly or join community based professionals.

Some parents will require more intensive help to improve their relationship with their child. Others will benefit from practical support and also planned respite periods from their child.

Parents who are suffering from a major psychiatric disorder may require referral to the adult mental health services. There may be others who would benefit from psychotherapeutic intervention because of their own early history of abuse and neglect. However, psychotherapy requires a considerable commitment and degree of emotional resilience; factors that are often absent in adults whose

Table 18.3 Factors influencing effects of abuse

Risk factors	Protective factors
• Abuse (note that often the child will experience more than one type of abuse): Type Severity Duration • Abuser: Especially if in parental role to child • Child: Early age at onset • Family functioning: Poor quality Unsupportive	• Child: Good coping style and skills Strengths – for example, in academic or sporting areas • Family functioning: Good quality of family relationships Presence of consistent, supportive adult in child's life (in or outside family) • Non-abusive parent(s): Supportive to child Believing the child (for example, in context of sexual abuse) Efforts to protect child from further risk Having support for themselves

emotional and interpersonal functioning have been damaged by maltreatment in childhood (Box 18.1).

Interventions for children

Treatment for the child should take account of several factors, including the child's symptoms, developmental stage, strengths, the type and context of the abuse, the degree of parental support, and current social circumstances.

- Common sequelae of all types of abuse are low self esteem, poor interpersonal relationships, and difficulties in trusting adults. It is important that all professionals who work with abused children are aware of this, not only those who may be providing specific therapeutic help but others such as teachers, youth workers,

---

paediatricians. This is for two reasons: firstly, it can help to explain some of the difficulties in engaging these children in activities, such as schoolwork, teamwork, and therapy. Secondly, spending time with the child can afford an opportunity to identify positive aspects of the child and boost self esteem, and also to form a trusting relationship.

- A consistent, supportive adult in the child's life will improve outcome.

Box 18.2 **Child sexual abuse**

Possible presentation
(Note, a third of children have no symptoms)
- Change in behaviour
- Social withdrawal
- Deterioration in schoolwork
- Sexualised behaviour
- Sleep disturbance
- Secondary enuresis or encopresis
- Fearfulness
- Panic attacks

In older children/adolescents
As above plus:
- Depression
- Self harming behaviours
- Running away
- Promiscuity
- Alcohol and drug abuse

Treatment (after child protection investigation)
Non-abusing parent(s)
- Education about sexual abuse and the grooming process
- Assessment of functioning of parent(s) and child before and after disclosure
- Reinforcement of competent parenting
- Advice on management of current or potential difficulties in the child

Child
- Not all children will require treatment from the CAMH team. However, indications are:
  – Moderate to severe symptoms
  – Risk of self harm
  – Poor parental support
- Treatment depends on the age of the child and the severity of symptoms
- Most children can be treated as outpatients

For children with moderate verbal ability and reasoning
- Abuse focused cognitive behaviour therapy
- Components include:
  – Education about sexual abuse
  – Education about protective strategies
  – Shifting the locus of blame for abuse from self to others
  – Identification of support
  – Coping strategies
  – Relaxation techniques
  – Treatment of depression
  – Treatment of symptoms of post-traumatic stress
  – Support for appearing in court

Box 18.1 **Key goals**

For the child
- Safe, nurturing environment
- Trusting relationship with a supportive adult
- Enhancement of resilience
- Reduction in symptoms

For the non-abusing parent
- Protectiveness
- Belief of and support for child
- Coping strategies
- Child behaviour management skills
- Treatment of mental health problems

For the abusing parent
(Note, involvement of CAMH team is often not appropriate)
- Other agencies aim to:
  Stop the abuse
  Invoke legal interventions
- Some abusing parents will have no or limited further contact with the child
- Some abusing parents will be referred to adult mental health services for:
  Treatment of mental health problems
  Treatment of substance misuse
  Treatment of poor impulse control

- It is helpful to encourage and promote particular strengths or skills the child may have.
- For children who have been sexually abused, the most effective treatment to date is abuse-focused cognitive behaviour therapy (CBT). If the non-abusing parent is involved in the treatment, the child's outcome is improved (Box 18.2).
- Group therapy, using the same principles, can be helpful.
- Some children who experience post-traumatic stress disorder may benefit from CBT or from eye movement desensitisation and reprocessing (EMDR).
- Play therapy may be helpful for younger children who are unable to articulate or understand their experiences and feelings.
- No controlled studies have been published on treatment for children who have witnessed domestic violence. The most widely described intervention is group counselling with a psycho-educational approach.
- Other treatments aimed at specific symptoms – for example, poor impulse control or poor peer relationships – may be of benefit but often need to be part of a more comprehensive package of intervention.
- More intensive treatment, as a day patient or inpatient, may be considered for the child and non-abusive parent.
- Children may sexually abuse other children. Some have a history of abuse and come from disturbed and chaotic family backgrounds. Children who abuse should be understood both as victims and offenders. Treatment for these children should be multi-agency and include advice for and consultation with others – for example, teachers – on how to respond to sexualised language and behaviours.

Consultation

At any stage in the process the child psychiatrist or team, or both, may offer consultation and advice to other agencies working in child protection – for example, helping them to gain an understanding of a child's presentation and how this might be managed. The child need not necessarily require psychiatric intervention.

Child protection is difficult and at times harrowing. Professionals may be traumatised by their work. The CAMH team can provide consultation and support to other agencies to try to minimise such effects.

Teaching and training

Input from child psychiatry to training of other professionals working with children and also to adult mental health professionals should include the short and long term effects of abuse and the care of its victims.

There should also be continuing training of those within the CAMH service to ensure maintenance and development of their assessment and therapeutic skills. There may be arrangements to allow training secondments of professionals from other agencies.

Policy planning

Specialists in child psychiatry should be involved in the development of local child protection policies and guidelines. As well as highlighting the need for support and treatment for some children and their non-abusing parents after the investigation, there is also a role in helping other agencies minimise the potentially traumatic impact of the investigative process.

Court work

Child psychiatrists may be called to court as expert or professional witnesses. They can inform the legal system about child development, the possible impact of abuse, and the child as a legal witness. CAMH clinicians can help promote optimum child oriented conditions for child witnesses.

Audit and research

Not all abused children and their parents require psychiatric intervention. It is important that further knowledge is gained about which interventions are most effective for which children and at what stage.

Prognosis

There is a wide range of possible outcomes. Some children, despite a history of abuse, gradually overcome their difficulties, lead healthy lives, and become loving parents. Sometimes an important role for the child psychiatrist is to help other agencies (and occasionally the CAMH team) to recognise that the prognosis for some children is poor, especially where there has been chronic, extensive abuse and neglect. For these children a realistic goal is the prevention of further emotional, social, and physical damage.

Further reading

Myers J, Berliner L, Briere J, Hendrix CT, Jenny C, Reid T, eds. *APSAC (American Professional Society on the Abuse of Children). Handbook on child maltreatment.* 2nd ed. Thousand Oaks, California: Sage, 2002.

Putnam FW. (2003) Ten-year research update review: child sexual abuse. *J Am Acad Child Adolesc Psychiatry* 2003;42:269–78.

Ramchandani P, Jones DPH. Treating psychological symptoms in sexually abused children. From research findings to service provision. *Br J Psychiatry* 2003;183:484–90.

Royal College of Psychiatrists. *Mental health and growing up.* (London: Royal College of Psychiatrists (series of factsheets).

CHAPTER 19

Medical Reports

Roy Meadow

Notification

A doctor who is worried that a child has been abused should telephone the local social work duty officer. If the case is urgent action may be required immediately. Always confirm the referral in writing within 24 hours. The letter, marked confidential, may be brief but should be written in language understandable to a non-medical person.

Medical reports

The courts require formal reports whenever medical evidence is being used in child abuse cases. Although the report may be requested by an instructing solicitor, one's over-riding duty is to the court – not the solicitor. Great care must be taken over the construction of the report so that fact and opinion are clearly distinguished (Box 19.1, Fig. 19.1). You may be questioned in court about the report. Usually, you are asked to address particular issues in detail, but quite often a doctor is asked in general terms for a "medical report."

Box 19.1 Report checklist

- Name
- Practising address
- Telephone numbers/fax number/email
- Professional position or appointments held
- Qualifications
- Relevant experience
- Confidentiality checked – authority for child's address to be disclosed?
- Welfare checklist – does the report take this into account?
- Documents seen
- List of people interviewed or consulted in connection with the report with appropriate details: times, dates, location
- List and details of examinations, assessments, and samples taken
- Chronology: check details of dates and times for accuracy
- Does the report refer to quoted comments from any interviews? If so, there is a contemporaneous note, and check that the report gives an accurate account of what the notes record?
- If the report is based on information provided by others, does the report make clear the nature of the information given, its source, the weight given to it, and the extent to which it has been relied on? Is there authority for disclosure of sources of information?
- Does the report make clear the basis on which opinion is given and conclusions are drawn?
- Has jargon been avoided?
- Where technical terminology is unavoidable, is it also explained in clear terms?
- Is the thinking process in the report clear and well reasoned?
- Have all possible alternatives – for example, of diagnosis, treatment, assessment – been explored and evaluated, and is this made clear in the report?
- Are there specific legal requirements that affect the report? If so, have they been met?
- List of exhibits referred to in the report . . . and are they attached?
- List of references cited, authorities quoted, or any other work relied on in the report; are copies, if appropriate, attached as exhibits, or will they be available for use in court?

Figure 19.1 One patient may have several sets of casenotes, each of which requires study. You may also be asked to study social services records and other reports.

In family proceedings a "letter of instruction" to an expert witness should have been jointly agreed by the parties, and approved by the court (Box 19.2). If the issues addressed are too narrow, too broad, or inappropriate for your knowledge or expertise, say so.

Format

The report should be typed on one side of paper in double spacing, "justified" on either side with wide margins. Number the paragraphs or sections consecutively so that they can be referred to easily during discussion or in giving evidence in court. Subheadings make it easier to read.

Affidavits

An affidavit is a statement of evidence set out in a standard format that has evolved over many years and is approved by the courts. It has to be sworn, or declared, before a commissioner for oaths or other authorised officer (which includes all solicitors) to whom a small fee is payable by the testifier.

Documents or copies of documents that are relevant to the case may become part of an affidavit as exhibits, and copies may be made for all the parties to the case and for the judge. If an expert is asked to prepare a report for a civil case the report (if it is to be used in evidence) will be put into the form of an affidavit by the solicitor for the party calling the expert witness and disclosed to the other side. The evidence may then be agreed, in which case the witness need not attend the trial and the affidavit can be read. Alternatively the evidence may not be agreed and the witness may be called to court to give oral evidence. Oral evidence of expert witnesses may then be limited to the reports that have been disclosed but not agreed, saving the court's time. Affidavits are not required in Children Act cases but may be used in other civil actions heard in the family court.

Joint investigations and police reports

Police and social services will jointly investigate some cases of child abuse. Social services may ask for a report for a child protection case conference. The police may ask for a report in the form of a witness statement, or they may ask for the report to be on their police report form, which is a cramped document. Most doctors prefer to write their report and to attach to it a brief declaration and signature on the official form. Sending the report by post allows more time for necessary thought and preparation. Under no circumstances should a doctor give in to pressure to prepare a report too hastily.

Writing a report for the police does not necessarily mean that a prosecution will follow. Once the police have completed their investigation into alleged criminal offences the file is submitted to the Crown Prosecution Service for consideration of the evidence and for legal advice. If the evidence is sufficient, the Crown Prosecution Service will conduct the case on behalf of the police.

The Director of Public Prosecutions has a different function. When certain serious criminal offences are suspected the director has the power to initiate an investigation into the matter and to authorise prosecution in the public interest.

Reports for criminal proceedings have their own format. The Crown Prosecution Service will advise on the requirements.

Box 19.2 **Reports for family courts**

The document should be headed:
- In the . . . . . . court
- Case Ref No . . . . . .
- Re . . . . . . (name of child, date of birth, age)

In the top right hand corner put:
- Filed on behalf of . . . . . .
- Statement No . . . . . .
- Date . . . . . .

And at the end add the following:
I declare that
1 We understand that our over-riding duty in written reports and giving evidence is to help the court on the matters within our expertise and we have complied with that duty.
2 We have set out in our report what we understand from those instructing us to be the questions in respect of which our opinion as experts is required.
3 We believe that the facts we have stated in this report are true and that the opinions we have expressed are correct. All of the matters upon which we have expressed our opinions lie within our field of expertise.
4 We have drawn the attention of the court to any matter of which we are aware which may affect the validity of our opinion.
5 Where there is a range of opinions on the matters with which the report deals, we have summarised the range of opinion and given reasons for the opinion.
6 We have stated the substance of all material instructions, whether written of oral, on the basis of which the report is written and we have indicated the sources of all information we have used if based on facts of which we have no personal knowledge.
7 Nothing has been included in this report, or excluded from it, that has been suggested to us by another party without our forming an independent view of it.
8 At the time of signing the report, we consider that it is complete, accurate and mentions all matters that we believe are relevant to our expressed opinion. We will notify those instructing us immediately and in writing if, for any reason, our existing report requires any correction or qualification.
9 We understand that:
   a Our report, subject to any correction before swearing as to its correctness, will form the evidence to be given under oath;
   b We may be cross examined on the report by a cross-examiner assisted by an expert;
   c We are likely to be the subject of adverse criticism by the judge if the court concludes that we have not taken reasonable care in trying to meet the standards set out above.
10 We confirm that we have not entered into any arrangement where the amount or payment of our fees is in any way dependent on the outcome of the case.
11 The report is provided to those instructing us with the sole purpose of assisting the court in this particular case. It may not be used for any other purpose, nor may it be disclosed to any third party, without our express written authority

Content of reports

- Do not give the child's address, school, or location or any information that would identify the child's foster carers or adoptive parents unless confidentiality has been first cleared with the court or the instructing advocate.

- At the start give your full name, current position, and medical qualifications. Follow that with some indication of previous relevant experience – for example, "I have been a principal in general practice for 12 years" or "I am a specialist registrar who has worked with children for five years." If you have had particular training or experience of child abuse mention its extent; if you have published research work on the subject say so. A curriculum vitae can be attached at the end of the report after the declaration.
- Make clear the nature of your involvement in the case in terms of how you came to encounter the child and how long you have been concerned with the case and in what capacity. State the extent of your knowledge of the case in terms of correspondence and discussion with colleagues and the nature of the documents and reports that you have seen. Sometimes many hospital records and documents will have been studied, in which case a statement such as "I have studied documents listed in the letter of instruction," may be sufficient.
- State the extent of your contact with the child – for example, "I examined the child in my outpatient clinic on 14 November 2006 and discussed the problems with the parents. The consultation lasted 50 minutes" or "I assessed the child every month during the following year, each assessment lasting about 15 minutes." Ensure that dates and times are accurate and keep careful records of all consultations, examinations, assessments, and discussions relating to the case.
- Summarise the case, being careful to simplify any medical jargon as the report will be read by many non-medical people and will probably be seen by the child's parents (Box 19.3). When relating the clinical history, write it down chronologically and, in addition to the date, make clear the child's age at each incident.
- Keep reports within your area of practice and knowledge.
- Clinical findings follow the history and should be set out in an ordered fashion. A diagram or photograph may be added to supplement the description. When the pattern of injury is typical – for example, finger marks showing a firm grip on a child or slap marks – an explanation of how and why that pattern is recognisable is helpful to lay people. Though the main findings may relate to a particular injury or to just one part of the body, always include a general appraisal of the child, including his or her height and weight (and their centile value) and, a note on the child's developmental abilities. This should be followed by a note of the child's

---

Box 19.3 Who sees reports?

- Reports are subject to the control of the courts. They are likely to be disclosed to all parties to the case
- In the *criminal court* the jury do not have copies of the medical/expert reports. Counsel, for prosecution and defence, select areas of the report as a basis on which to question the witness. The jury have to rely on what they hear in court
- In the *family court* the judge or magistrate has copies of all the reports and hears the doctor or other expert being questioned about it

---

Box 19.4 Meetings of experts

- In complex and contentious cases the medical experts may be asked to meet and identify areas of agreement and disagreement in advance of a family court hearing
- After such a meeting the participants may be asked to provide a further report or to sign an agreed joint statement

---

behaviour, whenever relevant, during the times that you have observed the child.

- The conclusion or opinion should be clear but should take into account other possible explanations and differential diagnoses. State the reasons for your opinion in the report, be prepared to discuss them subsequently, and to answer questions on relevant research, probability, and other issues. Any confirmatory pathological or radiological findings should be reported, explained, and interpreted.
- When providing an expert medical opinion in a report for court, ensure that all known relevant reasons leading to the conclusion and opinions given are included in the original statement and clearly set out. If additional information comes to light at a later stage, a supplementary report should be offered immediately. The courts may refuse to admit evidence of matters not contained in a statement filed with the court as the other parties will not have had a chance to consider or refute whatever is being postulated. In family proceedings the courts want to have all relevant information to help their decision.
- If you have seen a statement from another party that contradicts your opinion, finish your statement by making clear which of your findings are consistent with the contradictory statement and which are not, and why.
- You may be asked as an expert witness (if within your specialty) to include an explanation of child development, child behaviour, and the effect of adverse factors such as abuse on the child. If your opinion is based partially on research, then it should be cited. You are drawing attention to the particular needs of the child for the benefit of the court. You may be asked to consult with specified experts, or to interview relevant people or family members; and you may be provided with the court papers and asked to assess the evidence, to present an authoritative opinion (Box 19.4).

Access to records and reports

The Access to Health Records Act 1990 gives rights to individuals in relation to records held by health professionals about their physical or mental health. Computerised health records are covered by data protection legislation. The Access to Medical Reports Act 1988 gives qualified rights of access for individuals to medical reports prepared about them for employment or insurance purposes.

The Freedom of Information Act 2000 came into force in 2005, widening access to the personal information held about individuals. Basically, people have a right to know what has been said and written about them, unless the disclosure of that information would be detrimental to them, or certain specified exceptions to their right to disclosure apply. (See Bond T, Sandhu A (2005) for more information on access to clinical records.)

Further reading

Bond T, Sandhu A. *The therapist in court*. Sage: London, 2005

Burrows D. *Evidence in family proceedings*. Bristol: Jordan Publishing, 1999:207–13.

Children Act Advisory Committee. *Handbook of best practice in Children Act cases*. Section 5. London: Stationery Office, 1997.

Expert Witness Group. *The expert witness pack*. Bristol: Jordan Publishing 1997.

Royal College of Paediatrics and Child Health. *Child protection companion*. RCPCH: London, 2006.

Wall N. *Handbook for expert witnesses in children act cases*. Bristol: Jordan Publishing, 2000.

CHAPTER 20

Social Workers and Child Protection

Michael Preston-Shoot

The legislation, procedures, and terminology in this chapter reflect practice in England and Wales. Readers who work elsewhere will recognise the importance, philosophy, and principles of working together with other agencies when they are concerned about child abuse. They should be familiar with equivalent legislation procedures and terminology used in their country of practice

Councils with responsibilities for social services have four major child protection duties: to prevent children from experiencing ill treatment and neglect; to safeguard and promote the welfare of children in need; to investigate a child's circumstances when requested by a court; and (along with the National Society for the Prevention of Cruelty to Children (NSPCC)) to investigate information that a child is experiencing or is likely to experience considerable harm and decide whether any action should be taken to safeguard and promote the child's welfare. Each local authority has its own procedures but must work within the general framework of the Children Act 1989 and in accordance with government guidance. Councils with social services responsibilities therefore have a central role in the prevention, investigation, and management of cases of child abuse.

Organisational structures vary. Community based social workers are allocated work on the basis of geographical area, role, or specialism. Some councils also maintain hospital social work departments, where practitioners work with nominated wards, medical specialties, or consultants. Councils vary in the extent to which, after referral and initial investigation, hospital social workers are involved in child protection cases.

As a result of legislation (Health Act 1999; Health and Social Care Act 2001; Children Act 2004) new organisational structures are evolving. These "trusts" bring social services together with housing, health, and education in one agency.

In all work with children and families the child's welfare is paramount and is determined by consideration of a welfare checklist (section 1(3) of the Children Act 1989). Social work practice operates within this framework, which seeks to balance parental responsibility and rights with children's rights and the duty of the state to intervene in certain circumstances. Six principles inform such practice.

Primacy of family – This entails promoting the upbringing of children in need by their families when that is consistent with the duty to

Box 20.1 **Key practice skills, emphasising partnership**

- Honesty, openness, and respect
- Providing information about the purpose of interviews and available services
- Clear explanations of local authority powers and duties, reasons for concern, and what is or is not negotiable about involvement
- Clear language and preparation with families to enable their informed participation in decision making
- Engaging with the expression of strong feelings without defensiveness
- Addressing conflicts of interest directly, working with the family without compromising the child's interests
- Listening to families and understanding their perspective, without colluding with them, becoming overwhelmed, or maintaining unrealistic optimism
- Enabling family members and the child to contribute to important decisions
- Planning and reviews, to avoid drift and retain clear objectives
- Written agreements detailing the child's needs, the plan to meet these needs, the actions required by those involved, and the timescale
- Work addresses the family's concerns, values their contribution, and develops, when possible, their skills and strengths
- Infringing of a family's privacy only to the degree necessary to safeguard and promote the child's welfare
- Recording a detailed individual and family history, cross referenced with important events; the content and process of investigation, assessment, decision making, and intervention
- Decisions confirmed in writing
- Self awareness – monitoring the interaction between self and work, especially defence mechanisms such as avoidance of issue, defensive practice, and authoritarianism

safeguard and promote the child's welfare. Services may be provided to assist families – for instance, day care, family centres, and counselling. Courts will make orders only when they are satisfied that so doing would be better than making no order at all. Parents retain parental responsibility when a child is in care; the local authority is able to limit this only when necessary to safeguard and promote the child's welfare. Where practicable and appropriate children looked after by the local authority should be placed near the home or within the extended family, or both.

Figure 20.1 Counselling may be provided to help families. With permission from Jim Varney/Science Photo Library. Posed by models.

Partnership – This is the most effective means of providing care for children, whatever the legal position. It means the full involvement of parents *and* children in assessment, decision making, and reviews, drawing on their knowledge and understanding, an approach that should recognise different family structures (Box 20.1). One key feature is the negotiation of written agreements that detail the purpose and content of the work to be done. Another is the development of family group conferences.

Maintaining a focus on the child – This entails keeping the child fully informed, talking with them to learn their views about how to ensure their safety and wellbeing, and enabling them to understand how child protection procedures work. Cases must not be closed until social workers have spoken with the child and ensured their safety. Children must be seen within 24 hours of any allegation.

Multidisciplinary teamwork – No one professional group has all the knowledge and skills required for the prevention of abuse or neglect, for child protection, or for the work required after protection. Social workers may request assistance from other professionals working with children and families, who must assist unless this is unreasonable or prejudicial to the discharge of their own functions. The Children Act 2004 strengthens these duties to work together. All agencies concerned with the wellbeing of children must cooperate to improve children's outcomes in respect of health, safety, achievement, behaviour, employment, and training. This includes the early sharing of information.

Social workers must have the knowledge and skills to be able to question other professionals' opinions (Box 20.2). They must also review their files and meet other professionals when they receive referrals from them. Those involved in each case should agree a joint approach to investigation, information sharing with parents and children, and regular reviews of the work through discussion and supervision. Area child protection committees (to become local safeguarding children's boards as a result of the Children Act 2004) are responsible for developing agreed objectives and procedures for interagency cooperation in case management and decision making. This is crucial as interagency disagreements or conflicts between professionals undermine child protection work.

Antidiscriminatory practice – Local authority services and practice must not reflect or reinforce discrimination, myths, or stereotypes and must meet the special needs of particular groups. Thus when decisions are made about children, race, culture, religion, and linguistic background must be considered. Accordingly, work will target the impact of inequality and oppression on individuals and families. The power imbalance between clients and professionals will be challenged through the use of written agreements, client advocates, open records, informed participation in meetings, and attention to workers' sex, ethnicity, and use of power.

Prevention – An emphasis on abuse and child protection should not obscure other needs in a case nor the importance of provid-

---

Box 20.2 Registration of social workers

- To practise as a social worker, a practitioner must be registered with one of the four care councils in the United Kingdom
- When registered the social worker must uphold the code of conduct
- Breach of the code can lead to deregistration
- Registered practitioners must protect the rights and promote the interests of service users and carers, strive to establish and maintain their trust and confidence, and promote their independence while protecting them as far as possible from danger or harm
- Registered practitioners must be accountable for the quality of their work and take responsibility for maintaining and improving their knowledge and skills. They must uphold public trust and confidence in social care services and respect the rights of service users while seeking to ensure that their behaviour does not harm themselves or other people
- Social work employers are also bound by a code of conduct that includes providing training and development opportunities to enable practitioners to strengthen their skills and knowledge, and having policies and procedures for dealing with dangerous or discriminatory behaviour

---

Box 20.3 Risk assessment

By using agreed indicators of risk and levels of (important) harm the objective is to determine the seriousness, or likelihood, of risk or harm, or both. This must then be considered alongside possible interventions: balancing the effects of removing the child with the possibility of harm if he or she is not removed from the home and whether a voluntary agreement with the parents is sufficient to safeguard the child's welfare.

Low risk	Monitoring, with clear criteria when to act; ongoing assessment; negotiated agreement sought on work to be done; legal options considered if agreement is not possible
Potential risk Moderate risk Cumulative risk	Legal options to protect the child considered; agreement sought on work to be done; ongoing assessment
Acute/immediate risk	May warrant immediate removal of the child

Box 20.4 **Response to referrals**

- Social workers must decide within 24 hours what action to take, having clarified the nature of concerns about a child and understood the child's possible needs
- Possible evidence of criminal offences must be referred to the police, with whom social workers must cooperate in any subsequent investigation
- Discussions should be held with other agencies and with parents unless this would place a child at risk of harm
- Social workers have seven working days for an initial assessment of a child in need, including child protection cases
- They have a further 35 working days for a comprehensive assessment when the initial assessment concludes that children might be in need or face actual or likely risk of considerable harm
- In the latter instance, strategy discussions must be held, when agencies involved share information, to decide whether or not immediate protection of a child is necessary
- If concerns remain during or after assessment, a case conference must be held

Box 20.5 **Assessing prospects for rehabilitation**

Checklists have been developed to identify families in which the rehabilitation of abused children might be indicated. No checklist is foolproof. Care must be taken so that families are not oppressed by the inappropriate imposition of white Eurocentric norms and the exclusion of structural issues (such as racism, poverty, unemployment, and housing). Each case must be considered alongside the availability of research knowledge. The factors that must be included in this type of assessment include:
- What was the nature, frequency, and severity of the abuse or neglect?
- Has the abuse stopped? Is there a culture of violence or aggression in the family? How are relationships and decisions managed? How is power used?
- Do the parents accept responsibility and the need for change? Can they work for this change?
- Is there open communication about the abuse or neglect and about family problems? Are there substantial family problems? To what extent are the parents able to meet the child's needs? Is there a distinction between the child's needs and the parents' needs? Are expectations of children realistic?
- Can the child resist any abuse? Are supports available?
- Have the child's views been sought, worked with, and considered? Is the child fearful or requesting protection? Is the child accommodating to the abusing or neglectful parent?
- What has been the outcome of previous work with the family, if any?

ing services to children in need. Legal options should be the least coercive and consistent with meeting the child's needs, including no order at all. The state should intervene only in a manner that limits people's rights to the degree necessary to achieve the outcomes desired. Compulsory orders (emergency protection, child assessment, care orders) should be sought for the following reasons:

- When they are better than voluntary arrangements – that is, when services have been refused or failed, or are likely to fail, to promote the child's welfare; when there is serious risk; when assessment is frustrated
- When they are in the interests of the child – based on clearly identified needs
- After a detailed investigation and case conference that consider whether services by agreement with the family would meet the child's needs.

Emergency protection orders should not be the routine first step in response to child abuse except in instances of clear and serious risk of severe harm (Boxes 20.3 and 20.4).

More broadly, councils with social services responsibilities will, through liaison with other agencies and community groups, seek to develop community networks and resources to reduce environmental pressures and promote the prevention of abuse or neglect and the protection of children.

None the less, social workers face difficult dilemmas. These include prevention versus protection (at what level to intervene), care versus control (how to use the law), rights versus risk (when the state should intervene), and needs versus resources (what determines decisions). Effective supervision, training, guidelines, and multidisciplinary teamwork, together with knowledge of the law and good practice, are essential for decision making in this context.

Assessment and intervention

There should be open discussion between professionals and with children and parents. Social work practice has six interlocking components.

Acquisition and collation of information through facilitative questions, observation, listening and clarification, and informing decision making by placing risks to and needs of the child in the context of family history, important events, and details of abuse or neglect. Interviewing should be at the child's pace, restricting the number of interviews, ensuring the suitability of the work setting, and recording carefully. Creation of a safe space (reliability, consistency, role clarity) is essential if those involved are to provide information and to convey their feelings and experiences. Social workers will look for evidence that corroborates statements of abuse or neglect. They must avoid preconceptions and exerting undue influence on people to disclose.

Study and evaluation of information – This entails distinguishing fact from opinion and content (the "what") from process (how people have engaged with the issues), using research and theoretical knowledge, and considering the case from different perspectives. The task is to understand and appraise the available information. For instance, what is the effect of parental behaviour on the child? What awareness is there in the family of the child's needs? What networks are available to support this family? How cooperative have the parents been with professionals?

Formulation of assessment – This entails defining and clarifying problems and weighing up risks, needs, and resources. A needs assessment focuses on the child and the family, with special reference to the child's health and development (physical and mental health,

Box 20.6 **Family group conferences**

- Immediate and wider family members meet to find solutions to concerns, using their experience, knowledge, and skills
- The family defines who is in the family, possibly including friends and community members
- Meetings focus on planning and decision making in response to concerns and issues presented by professionals as arising from a comprehensive assessment
- Professionals should clearly delineate what is non-negotiable from their perspective and what falls within the family's scope for decision making, and what resources they can make available
- Family group conferences do not replace child protection conferences but may facilitate the management of cases in which planning is required to ensure the welfare of a child in need or to develop and implement a child protection plan

Box 20.8 **Supervision and management of child protection**

- Includes a detailed study of case files
- Ensures that procedures and statutory guidance on good practice are followed
- Ensures that information is exchanged between agencies and that action taken in response to referrals and assessment is documented
- Focuses on the process and content of assessment, using statutory guidance; considers the implications of race, culture, and other social divisions for case management; and analyses the information collected against knowledge informed by research on child care, health, and development
- Ensures that child protection plans are developed, implemented, and reviewed

and social, emotional, educational, physical, and behavioural development) and environmental stresses (housing, income, race, and social and community networks). Resource assessment includes those resources available to the family and those within the professional network that might enable risks to be decreased, problems resolved, and needs met. An initial investigation and assessment will consider the sources and levels of risk or harm, or both, and the grounds for concern, culminating in recommendations of how best to protect the child, including the legal options most likely to promote this. When an investigation and assessment rule out abuse or neglect, everyone involved must be informed in writing and services offered to children in need and their families. A comprehensive assessment, when requested by a court or case conference to provide the basis for decisions about the future management of the case, will gather and evaluate information on the areas of concern: the child's health and development; the family's resources, strengths, and problems; family interactions and the ability to meet the child's needs; and available support networks. Recommendations will be made about what needs to change to reduce the risk to the child or meet his or her needs, or both, and what form of intervention is most likely to achieve this (Box 20.6).

Child protection plan – This should include the child's needs (including education, health, and culture); how these needs are to be met; services to be provided, including placements, with their aims and timescales; arrangements for contact between the child and the family; arrangements for consulting the child, parents, and significant others and how they are to be involved in decision making; responsibility for implementing the plan; contingency plans if the plan or placement breaks down; and review dates.

Intervention with individuals (child, non-abusing parent, perpetrator) or families, or both. Therapeutic work may entail play therapy with children, family therapy, or the use of group work with survivors or perpetrators of abuse. The objectives of intervention may be to decrease the risks of abuse or neglect, to improve an individual's or family's strengths and resources, or to work through the effects of abuse or neglect. Intervention, when a child has been removed from home, may aim to test the prospects for rehabilitation or, if return home has been excluded, to work towards a permanent placement. The first six weeks are crucial in the consideration of rehabilitation or permanent placement if work is to remain focused and purposeful (Box 20.5).

Review – This entails involving parents, children, and others involved in the case to evaluate progress, to reconsider the child protection plan and whether any change is necessary in the child's legal status, and to establish the framework and content of forthcoming work to safeguard and promote the child's welfare (Boxes 20.7 and 20.8). Written notification of the outcome must be given to those involved in the case. Reviews demonstrate that assessment is an ongoing process involving the child, family, and professional network.

Contact

The frequency and length of contact between social workers and families vary. During initial investigations it can be daily for several hours. When meetings between children looked after by the local authority and their parents are supervised it can amount to several times each week over a considerable period. Frequency and length of contact at the assessment and intervention stages will vary considerably depending on the method and focus of the work. Concerns exist that social workers are under-resourced; in particular that the time involved in initial investigations, child protection assessments, recording, and court work limits resources for intervention after assessment or work with children and families when need rather than abuse is the focus.

Box 20.7 **Teamwork and information sharing**

- To safeguard and promote the welfare of the child requires professionals and others to share information about children and their parents
- The needs of the child must be paramount
- Information sharing should take place within protocols agreed between agencies responsible for, or with some involvement in, child protection
- Confidential information may be disclosed to safeguard children and to prevent and/or detect crime

Further reading

Department of Health. *Child protection. Messages from research*. London: HMSO, 1995.

Department of Health. *Framework for the assessment of children in need and their families*. London: Stationery Office, 2000.

Department of Health. *The challenge of partnership in child protection: practice guide*. London: HMSO, 1995.

Department of Health. *What to do if you're worried a child is being abused*. London: DoH, 2003. www.dh.gov.uk/assetRoot/04/06/13/03/04061303.pdf

Laming H. *Inquiry into the death of Victoria Climbié*. London: Stationery Office, 2003.

CHAPTER 21

Case Conferences

Michael Preston-Shoot

The legislation, procedures, and terminology in this chapter reflect practice in England and Wales. Readers who work elsewhere will recognise the importance, philosophy, and principles of working together with other agencies when they are concerned about child abuse. They should be familiar with equivalent legislation procedures and terminology used in their country of practice

Case conferences are central to assessment, interagency cooperation, and decision making in child protection. Social services departments (and sometimes the NSPCC) convene them when an initial investigation has confirmed, or suspected, abuse or neglect. Their decisions must take account of all the available information, including a detailed individual and family history with relevant events and an evidence based, knowledge informed appraisal of the family's ability to protect the child and willingness to cooperate with professionals.

Except for registration and the appointment of a key worker, case conferences make recommendations to participant agencies, which should follow locally agreed procedures for confirming their intention to implement them. Key workers and local authority or NSPCC social workers may not be those most in contact with the family but will ensure that child protection plans are developed and implemented. They are central to interagency work: coordinating agency contributions to assessment, intervention, and review; engaging the child and parents in the child protection plan; and facilitating communication between agencies (Boxes 21.1–21.7).

Confidentiality

Effective intervention and case management depend on consideration of all available information. Child protection inquiries commonly pinpoint the failure to disclose or ask for information as crucial in distorting assessment and decision making. Consequently, the Children Act 2004 created provision for shared databases to support information exchange between agencies about children in need and children experiencing or likely to experience severe harm. All those involved with children's wellbeing must ensure that they take account of the need to safeguard and promote the welfare of children – for example, by early sharing of information.

The Data Protection Act 1998 allows disclosure of information without an individual's consent to prevent or assist with the detec-

Box 21.1 **Tasks of case conferences**

- To share and coordinate information and concerns about the child and family, to assess the severity of abuse and neglect, to assess the likelihood of severe harm in the future, to evaluate the degree of risk, and to decide what action is necessary to safeguard and promote the child's welfare
- To fulfil statutory obligations for the protection of children
- To formulate an agreed, recommended plan of management and intervention that addresses the abuse or neglect, risks, and needs with the child's welfare and safety the paramount aim. This must include consideration of what legal action is necessary to protect the abused or neglected child and other children in the family and what services should be provided on the basis of assessed needs
- To analyse information about the child's developmental needs and the capacity of the parents.
- To decide whether to place the child's name on the child protection register and to nominate a key worker
- To agree if and when a child protection review is required – no more than six months from the case conference at which the child's name was placed on the register
- To make judgements based on evidence

tion of crime. Case law recognises that children will be safeguarded only if professionals exchange information. The right to privacy (Article 8, European Convention of Human Rights) is qualified and gives way to the higher order principle of safeguarding and promoting the welfare of the child.

Codes of confidentiality issued by the General Medical Council, the British Association of Social Workers, and the Nursing and Midwifery Council allow disclosure and confirm the duty to share information when there is reason to believe a person is being abused or that serious danger exists. The protection of the child is paramount.

Composition of case conferences

Participants in case conferences include those with specific responsibilities for child protection and those with a contribution to make to the specific case.

- *The chairperson* is a senior member of the children's services department with detailed knowledge and understanding of child protection and without current or past line management respon-

Figure 21.1 Teachers may be the first to whom a child discloses abuse. With permission from Martin Riedl/Science Photo Library. Posed by models.

sibility for the case. When possible the same person should chair all case conferences concerning particular children and families. The chairperson ensures the conference puts the child's interests first, clarifies the meeting's purpose and the roles of people present, and enables each person to contribute verbally and by reports. The chairperson should meet the child and family beforehand to ensure their understanding of the conference's purpose and procedures (Box 21.2).

- *NSPCC* – Some staff attend as observers or consultants when they are not directly involved in the case. They may provide comprehensive assessments to inform decision making or resources such as family centres and family therapy.
- *Social workers and team leaders* report on the initial investigation and assessment. They provide information on important events, concerns about the child's safety and the ability of the parents, past and present child development, and the expressed views of children and their parents. They are responsible for ensuring that everyone with a relevant contribution to make has been invited; and they collate and record all available information.
- *Education welfare officers* are sometimes concerned directly in an investigation or can provide information about the family, or both, especially regarding school attendance and performance.

- *Teachers, nursery and playgroup workers, and childminders* often observe symptoms of abuse or neglect; they may be the first to whom a child discloses abuse (Fig. 21.1).
- *The police* will provide information on any suspected individual discussed at the conference and, when officers have worked with social workers in the initial investigation, will report on their assessment after interviews with the child, parents, or other people concerned. Serious assault or abuse or neglect should be reported so that officers can investigate and consider prosecution.
- *General practitioner* – Whether or not concerned directly in the initial investigation, the general practitioner may have important knowledge of the child and family.
- *Paediatricians*, working in a hospital or the community, are sometimes the first to suspect or identify abuse or neglect. They will advise on diagnosis and on whether the signs and symptoms are attributable to the parents or carers.
- *Health visitors, school nurses, hospital nurses, and nurse managers* contribute knowledge of the child and family. They may contribute to the child protection plan, especially when this entails monitoring a child's health and development.
- *Probation officers* may work with family members or can provide information about previous or possible involvement with the family (for example, work with offenders or marital work).
- *Voluntary organisations* may be involved when they provide or could offer services to children and families.
- *Armed services* may also be involved.

The circumstances of the case may indicate the involvement of current or former foster parents or residential social workers, and other agencies or professionals: the local authority housing department, especially in cases of rent arrears, overcrowding, or questions of homelessness; the Department of Social Security, where financial difficulties are relevant; and psychiatrists and practitioners working with learning disabled people.

Specialist advice must be available to case conferences, such as lawyers from the local authority's legal section and interpreters and specialists working with disabled people and people from minority ethnic groups. Their role is to contribute to informed decision making – for example, about legal options and the cultural components of a case. Once a court has granted an emergency protection or interim care order and appointed a children's guardian, this officer of the court, who advises the court on issues of case management, represents the interests of the child, and provides courts with an independent social work perspective, may attend as an observer.

Parental attendance

Parents and children must be invited to attend case conferences unless the chairperson decides that their exclusion is justified – for children because of their age and understanding; for parents when attendance would preclude proper consideration of the child's interests. This includes the likelihood of the conference being disrupted, violence towards professionals or the child, or undue influence being exerted by parents on a child. It does not include the possibility of prosecution. The reasons for exclusion should be recorded in the child's file.

When the interests of parents and children conflict, the child's interests have priority. If parents and children are not present the conference must receive or ask for a report of their views (a written report, statement, or audio tape) and ensure that they receive details of discussions and recommendations.

Local child protection procedures, agreed by local safeguarding childrens boards, will detail how parental and child attendance,

ideally for the entire conference (though separate attendance may be necessary) should be facilitated. Including parents and children exemplifies the Children Act's commitment to partnership and requires professionals to address envisaged problems, such as sharing confidential information, through training and procedural preparations. The following can encourage meaningful family participation:

- Partnership underpinning all work with the family – openness, consultation, and consideration of wishes and views expressed
- Leaflets on the nature and purpose of case conferences
- Training for professionals
- Preparatory work with children and parents on their contribution to case conferences
- Assistance to facilitate attendance – for example, timing, venue, fares, and creche facilities
- Enabling parents and children to bring an advocate to support and advise them
- Written reports from professionals that distinguish facts from observations from opinions
- Active chairing – introducing the participants, clarifying purposes, and ensuring language is "client friendly"
- Open discussion about the nature and degree of risks and the resources required, including those from the family, to implement the recommended plan
- Provision of minutes and written notification of decisions and recommendations, with follow-up to clarify any outstanding issues. Minutes should contain details of the unresolved issues of child protection, the interagency work necessary to deal with these, and how the child protection plan is related to the identified needs and risks.

Core group meetings and child protection reviews

Initial case conferences agree outline child protection plans.

Core group meetings, which must initially start within 10 working days of the case conference, develop, finalise, and implement the child protection plan based on the comprehensive assessment. Core group meetings will change the plan when necessary, by considering current risks and needs in the family and whether the plan continues to protect the child. The frequency of meetings will be determined by the complexity of the case. Membership will comprise those with essential contributions to the child's welfare.

Child protection reviews evaluate interagency cooperation and consider if registration should be continued or terminated. The

Box 21.7 **Government policy guidance requires that work in child protection is:**

- Child centred
- Rooted in child development
- Focused on outcomes for the child
- Evidence based
- Based on assessment as a continuous process not an event
- Focused on, and able to build upon, the child's and the family's strengths
- Multi-agency

usual interval between these reviews will be six months, but anyone may request a review at any time. The first review will be three months after the case conference. The same requirements concerning parental and child attendance apply.

Statutory reviews

When children are being looked after by the local authority *statutory reviews* are required after the first four weeks, three months, and every six months thereafter. They may be combined with child protection reviews. Parents and children are invited to attend, separately when this is indicated, with an officer of the social services department (not the social worker or team leader) responsible for coordinating the review and reports, including annual health reports. The local authority is required to consult and consider the views of the child, parents, and other people relevant to the case, including healthcare professionals. The child's views about the attendance of professionals at these reviews must be considered. Each review must reappraise the plan for the child, including case objectives, any variations to the child's placement, legal status, contact with family, and education and health needs. A formal record is made and the results sent to those concerned in the case.

Local safeguarding childrens boards

The role of local safeguarding childrens boards, outlined by the Children Act 2004 and building on the work of area child protection committees may be described as follows:

Box 21.8 **Children and Family Court Advisory and Support Service (CAFCASS)**

- CAFCASS provides independent representation for children in specific proceedings relating to:
  - Children Act 1989
  - Adoption and Children Act 2002
  - Human Fertilisation and Embryology Act 1990
  - Crime and Disorder Act 1998
- CAFCASS works only in the family courts, and commonly represents the child, as "children's guardian" in supervision or care order proceedings

- To determine and evaluate arrangements for working together – developing clear policies on roles and responsibilities in prevention, assessment, investigation, and treatment of child abuse and neglect; and publishing these procedures, including the principle of including parents and children at all conferences
- To agree objectives and performance indicators for child protection
- To develop and review joint training – covering assessment, investigation, and treatment; issues of race and sex; children with disabilities; how feelings about abuse affect practice; and professional stereotypes
- To encourage and review interagency cooperation, including the development of protocols on child protection investigations, on resolving disagreements between agencies, and child and parental attendance at conferences and decision making meetings
- To evaluate working together in the light of local and national evidence of best practice
- To develop and review arrangements for expert advice
- To review and when necessary inquire into cases when a child has died or been seriously harmed
- To monitor case conferences and the implementation of legal procedures
- To publish an annual report and to raise community awareness of the need to safeguard children.

The core membership comprises senior officers or professionals, with delegated decision making powers, from the social services and education departments, NSPCC, police, probation service, health services, and representatives from armed services (when appropriate); and CAFCASS (Box 21.8), drug and alcohol services and youth offending teams. Other agencies that may be involved include voluntary organisations, housing departments, the Department of Social Security, and those with particular skill, for instance in religious, ethnic, and cultural matters.

CAFCASS – the Children and Family Court Advisory and Support Service (www.cafcass.gov.uk)
NSPCC – the National Society for the Prevention of Cruelty to Children (www.nspcc.org.uk)

The representatives pass reports and recommendations to their own agencies and inform the local safeguarding childrens board of their agency's work in child protection.

Further reading

Department of Health. *Framework for the assessment of children in need and their families.* London: Stationery Office, 2000.

HM Government. *Working together to safeguard children. A guide to interagency working to safeguard and promote the welfare of children,* 2006: www.everychildmatters.gov.uk/resources-and-practice/IG00060/

Laming H. *Inquiry into the death of Victoria Climbié.* London: Stationery Office, 2003.

Reder P, Duncan S, Gray M. *Beyond blame – child abuse tragedies revisited.* London: Routledge, 1993.

Reder P, Duncan S. *Lost innocents. A follow-up study of fatal child abuse.* London: Routledge, 1999.

CHAPTER 22

Child Care Law

Barbara Mitchels

The legislation, procedures, and terminology in this chapter reflect practice in England and Wales. Readers who work elsewhere will recognise the importance, philosophy, and principles of working together with other agencies when they are concerned about child abuse. They should be familiar with equivalent legislation procedures and terminology used in their country of practice

Child abuse can be physical, sexual, or emotional. Just as forms of abuse or neglect vary, so do the needs of each child and their family. The Children Act 1989 (Children Act) embodies principles of cooperation and negotiation between professionals and families in child protection, imposing a duty on local authorities to provide a wide range of assistance and services for children in need and their families (Box 22.1). The family court comprises three tiers, the High Court, the County Court, and the Family Proceedings Court, each with concurrent jurisdiction (Fig. 22.1). Cases can move up or down the tiers as necessary. The Children Act has subsidiary legislation, rules, case law, and guidance, indicating how its provisions are to be implemented.

Principles of the Children Act

Non-intervention

The Children Act encourages negotiation and cooperation between parents, children and professionals, enabling children, wherever possible, to remain within their own families with an appropriate input of resources rather than removing them from home. The Children Act contains a range of private and public law orders, giving the court a wide choice of possibilities with which to meet the needs of a child, but an order should not be made unless it is better for the child than making no order at all. The court has to ask itself the question "Do we need to make an order to safeguard this child's health and welfare?".

Avoidance of delay

Delay is contrary to the interests of the child and should be avoided

Box 22.1 **Principles underpinning the Children Act 1989**

• Non-intervention   • Avoidance of delay
• The paramount importance of the welfare of the child

Figure 22.1 Paths of appeal in family cases.

unless constructive and absolutely necessary. Courts control timing and evidence through 'directions hearings' in which formal agreement is reached about parties, notice, filing and service of evidence and reports, and dates of future hearings. Expert witnesses therefore need to inform the court of dates when they are available to carry out assessments and to give evidence. In relation to expert assessments and reports, the directions given may also cover funding, instructions, disclosure of information, consent issues, venue of medical or psychiatric examinations, who will accompany a child, and the person(s) to whom the results should be given.

Welfare of the child

The welfare of the child is the paramount consideration for the court. The Children Act contains a welfare checklist setting out issues to which the court must have regard in making decisions about

Box 22.2 **Welfare checklist**

(From section 1(3) of the Children Act 1989)
• The ascertainable wishes and feelings of the child concerned (considered in the light of his age and understanding)
• His physical, emotional, and educational needs
• The likely effect on him of any change in his circumstances
• His age, sex, background, and any characteristics of his that the court considers relevant
• Any harm that he has suffered or is at risk of suffering
• How capable are each of his parents, and any other person in relation to whom the court considers the question to be relevant, in meeting his needs
• The range of powers available to the court under this Act in the proceedings in question

care, supervision, contact, and certain contested private law orders. Court reports should take into account the principles of the welfare checklist (Box 22.2).

Children cannot always be sufficiently objective to know what is best for them, therefore their wishes and feelings cannot form the sole basis for the court's decision, but a child's views should be ascertained and taken seriously. Even very young children can indicate feelings by non-verbal means, but skill is required in interpretation. The courts may be assisted in their decisions by expert evidence and by officers from the Children and Family Court Advisory and Support Service (CAFCASS) – for example, the children's guardian in care cases, whose task is to advise the court of the child's wishes and feelings and recommend to the court the action most appropriate to safeguard and promote the welfare of the child.

Parental responsibility

> Parental responsibility always belongs to the mother of a child and to the natural (birth) father provided he is married to the mother at the time of the birth, or marries her subsequently. Their parental responsibility can be shared, but only lost by death or adoption.

The Children Act created the concept of "parental responsibility," defined in section 3(1) as "all the rights, duties, powers, responsibilities and authority which by law the parent of a child has in relation to a child and his property." Parental responsibility is the legal basis for making decisions about a child, including consent for medical treatment. More than one person can have parental responsibility for a child at the same time. However, not all parents have parental responsibility for their children.

Mothers and married fathers – Every mother of a child born to her (married or not), and the father who is married to the child's mother at the time of or subsequent to their child's birth, automatically has parental responsibility for their child; it can be shared with others, but will be lost only by death or adoption.

Unmarried fathers – Unmarried fathers may acquire parental responsibility for their child in one of several ways:

- From 1 December 2003, an unmarried father automatically acquires parental responsibility for his child if, with his consent and that of the child's mother, he is named as the child's father on the registration of the child's birth. This law does not operate retrospectively
- By formal "parental responsibility agreement" signed by the mother and father, appropriately witnessed, then registered. Copies may be obtained for a fee, in the same way as a birth certificate

> Box 22.3 **Parental responsibility can be acquired by a birth father by**
>
> - Registration as the father on the child's birth certificate with consent of the mother
> - Parental responsibility agreement
> - A court order for parental responsibility
> - Parental responsibility awarded by the court – for example, along with a residence order

- A court may make an order awarding parental responsibility to the father if this is consistent with the interests of the child (Box 22.3).

Acquisition of parental responsibility by others – Parental responsibility may be awarded along with a residence or guardianship order. A local authority acquires parental responsibility for a child under a care order and limited parental responsibility under an emergency protection order.

There is an additional provision in section 3(5) of the Act that those without parental responsibility may "do what is reasonable in all the circumstances to safeguard and promote the welfare" of a child in their care – for example, allowing a baby sitter, or relative, to take a child in their care for medical help in an emergency.

> Removal of parental responsibility:
> Parental responsibility gained by an agreement or by a court order may be removed by the court if necessary in the interests of the child

Child protection referrals

Practitioners who suspect abuse, or are concerned about the health or safety of a child, should refer their concerns about the child to the

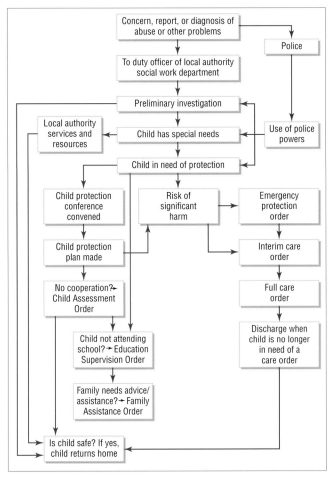

Figure 22.2 Child protection procedures.

local social services duty officer or to the local authority legal department (Fig. 22.2). Referrals should be confirmed in writing within 24 hours. In emergencies, the police may be notified and requested to use their powers under the Children Act. Local and national guidelines set out the policy, protocols, and procedures for interdisciplinary cooperation in child protection in each area. Guidance (DoH 1999) provides authoritative information on procedure, including the administration and conduct of child protection conferences. These are interdisciplinary conferences, convened by the local authority in cases of concern and designed to investigate a child's circumstances and assess the need for a child protection plan. If practitioners are asked to give information for a child protection conference, a report should be provided, particularly if the practitioner is unable to attend. Advice and information regarding local child protection procedures including child protection conferences can be sought from the social services or legal department of the local authority.

Medical or psychiatric examination or assessment of children

Who can give consent?

In all cases, any person with parental responsibility for the child may give consent; or the child may give consent if he or she is of sufficient age and understanding (Box 22.4). Under the Family Law Reform Act 1969, at 16 a child has the right to consent to medical treatment, examination, or assessment. The House of Lords Case, *Gillick v West Norfolk and Wisbech Area Health Authority [1986] AC 112*, settled that, below this age, competence to give consent is a matter of professional judgment based on the child's individual age, ability, the nature and seriousness of the decision to be made, and the levels of information given. The practitioner may act on the consent of a child of sufficient age and ability, of a person with parental responsibility for the child, or an order of the court.

Medical and psychiatric assessment and treatment

When a child needs medical or psychiatric examination or treatment, doctors must either obtain the appropriate consent or, in the absence of consent, seek a court order, usually through the legal department of the local authority to the High Court or in child protection proceedings.

Box 22.4 **Who can give consent to medical examination and treatment for a child**

- Any person with parental responsibility for the child
- The child, if over the age of 16
- The child, if under 16 years but has sufficient age and understanding
- This will depend on:
  The child's age
  The child's level of understanding
  The nature and seriousness of the decision to be made
  The information given to the child
- The High Court may give a declaratory order regarding medical examination or treatment where consent is in issue

---

Examinations carried out without such consent could constitute an assault and could render the practitioner liable for assault in civil or criminal law, or both.

For guidance on the appropriate action in medical emergencies where consent is not available, refer to the GMC, BMA or hospital legal advisors, or the local authority legal team.

When a child is clearly too young or otherwise incapable of making their own medical decisions, consent for medical or psychiatric examination and treatment lies with those who have parental responsibility for the child, subject to the over-riding jurisdiction of the High Court.

Understanding the potential consequences of consenting to or refusing treatment or assessment increases with age and maturity, the child's intelligence and level of understanding, influenced by the detail of the information provided. The Department of Health's *Reference Guide to Consent for Examination or Treatment* recommends that doctors should record factual information given to the child, including questions asked and the child's responses, for possible reference later if the child's ability to make the decision were to be questioned. When a child is seen alone, efforts should be made to obtain the child's agreement to inform their parents, except when this is clearly not in the child's best interests.

If a child is reluctant or fearful, or is resisting treatment, doctors should work in cooperation with the child's parents or carers to resolve the child's fears and to facilitate the treatment by persuasion rather than coercion, acting always in the best interests of the child and bearing in mind the child's emotional wellbeing in addition to the child's physical care.

Child's right to refuse examinations and assessments

A child may make an informed decision to refuse a medical examination or assessment. A child's ability to refuse will depend on factors including age and understanding, and also on the information given. Practitioners should ensure that a child who is competent to make a decision is given an age-appropriate explanation of what is proposed and the potential consequences of refusal (Box 22.5). A note should be made of the information given to the child and of the substance of the questions and answers on which the practitioner's assessment of the child's capability to make decisions is based. That note may be required later in court if the child's capability is questioned. In court proceedings for care, supervision, child assessment, or emergency protection, a Children's Guardian should be appointed at an early stage. They will ascertain the child's views. When a child is brought to the doctor in accordance with a direction of the court, but then refuses, the examination should not proceed and the matter should be referred back to the court.

What if consent is refused?

Distinguish necessary medical treatment from medical examinations for purely forensic purposes.

If a doctor considers that medical examination or treatment is clinically necessary for a child and consent is refused, or those with parental responsibility for the child disagree with each other or with the child who is of sufficient age to give consent, then the doctor should immediately inform the hospital social services department

Box 22.5 **Action if a child refuses consent for medical examination or treatment:**

- Reassure the child
- Discuss in age-appropriate way and answer child's questions
- Where appropriate, seek consent from person with parental responsibility
- If child is Gillick competent or over 16, seek legal advice and, if necessary, obtain an order from the court.
- If forensic examination required in the context of court proceedings, refer matter back to the court

Box 22.6 **An important point to remember**

In cases involving children, a distinction must be made at the outset between examinations and assessments for medical diagnosis and treatment and those that are purely for forensic purposes.
If there is an element of both – for example, where a child has been violently sexually abused and a first immediate examination is required to ascertain whether there are resulting internal injuries, sexually transmitted disease, or pregnancy – then the matter may be treated as a medical necessity in addition to its potential forensic use.

and the legal department of their local authority, who will advise (Box 22.6). They may seek an appropriate court order. The High Court, for example, may give a declaration that it is lawful for the doctor to treat the child. In some circumstances, an emergency protection order or a care order may be appropriate.

When immediate emergency treatment is required, medical practitioners may rely on their own clinical judgment if those in a position to give consent are unavailable. See the General Medical Council, British Medical Association, or workplace guidance on medical emergencies.

If in an emergency, treatment of a child is necessary but consent has been refused, the doctor should immediately contact the hospital social services department or the duty social services officer of the local authority and an emergency court order may be obtained. There is a judicial 'out of hours' service available at all times and in an emergency, magistrates and judges may make an order by telephone.

In some cases, High Court judges have said that they will protect a child who is under the age of 18 by authorising medical treatment when doctors deem it necessary, even though the child has refused. The judges take the view that, while they have jurisdiction and are able to protect the child, they will do so. Once the child has reached the age of majority, at 18, however, if they have the mental capacity to make their own decisions, the courts are unlikely to intervene.

Control by courts of examinations for purely forensic purposes

Under no circumstances should a practitioner proceed in an examination or assessment of a child for purely forensic purposes without appropriate leave of the court.

Repeated medical and psychiatric examinations for forensic purposes can cause a child unnecessary stress. The Children Act and its subsidiary rules empowers the court in the context of proceedings for emergency protection, child assessment, interim care, and supervision to regulate such examinations and make appropriate directions, which may include nomination of the specific practitioner(s) to carry out the examination or assessment, the venue, those to be present, and those to whom the results may be given. The court will usually also give directions for disclosure of information (for example, relevant court papers or other medical or psychiatric evidence) to the expert when it may assist diagnosis, treatment advice, or prognosis.

Breaches of these rules are viewed seriously, and any evidence obtained without compliance with the rules may be disallowed in court.

Emergency protection order

The court will grant an emergency protection order (EPO) if it is satisfied that there is reasonable cause to believe that a child is likely to suffer significant harm unless removed from their present accommodation (or, alternatively, not kept at their present accommodation). Anyone may apply, but the usual applicant is the local authority. This order could operate to remove a child at risk of harm from home or to keep a child safely in hospital. Local authorities have additional grounds if they cannot gain access to a child who might be suffering significant harm. The order lasts eight days initially, with the possibility of a further extension of seven days only. It may be granted without notice. There is no appeal but after 72 hours it may be challenged in specified circumstances.

On application for an EPO, the court appoints a Children's Guardian for the child, giving directions as necessary for entry and search, disclosure of the child's whereabouts, medical examinations, and contact. Police or medical practitioners may be asked to help in carrying out the order. The child, who may be looked after in local authority accommodation or hospital, must be returned home as soon as it becomes safe to do so. If necessary, renewal or another protective order must be sought before the EPO expires.

If a child is in hospital, then the retention of the child in the hospital and the sharing of parental responsibility by the local authority under the EPO with the parents will facilitate any necessary medical examinations or treatment, subject to the directions of the court.

Police powers of removal of child

The police have power under the Children Act to remove a child to suitable accommodation for 72 hours or to prevent a child's removal from a safe place when there is reasonable cause to believe that the child would otherwise be likely to suffer significant harm. The police may intervene to ensure that a child in need of care is taken from home to hospital or another safe place or to prevent the removal of a child, for example, when someone with parental responsibility is attempting to remove the child from hospital. The 72 hour duration allows time for further investigation of the child's circumstances and for an emergency court order to be sought where necessary.

Note that this provision, sometimes colloquially referred to by social workers as a "PPO," is a power and not a court order, and it does not confer parental responsibility on the police or the local authority.

Box 22.7 **The practical effect of care orders**

- Local authority gains parental responsibility
- A care plan must be in place for the child
- The child is subject to regular reviews
- The child may be removed from home if necessary for his or her welfare
- Contact with family and others may be controlled by the court and local authority
- The care order may exist until the child reaches 18, unless it is discharged earlier
- On leaving care, the child is entitled to special help

Box 22.8 **The practical effect of supervision orders**

- Orders last for up to one year
- May be renewed, to a maximum of three years total
- Directions may be made with supervision orders
- Medical assessment or treatment, or both, may be the subject of directions, subject to consents
- No changes in parental responsibility

Care and supervision orders

There is now only one way for a child to be taken into statutory care. The court must be satisfied that the grounds laid down in section 31 of the Children Act are met and an order is necessary to safeguard the child. Care orders may subsist until a child reaches 18 or they may be discharged earlier (Box 22.7). Supervision orders may be made for one year, with possible extensions for up to one year at a time, to a maximum of three years (Box 22.8).

The grounds for care and supervision are the same, and only a local authority or an authorised person or organisation (currently the NSPCC) may apply. The court must have regard to the welfare checklist, the principles of non-intervention and avoidance of delay, and be satisfied that:
- The child concerned is suffering or likely to suffer significant harm
- That the harm, or likelihood of harm, is attributable to:
  The care being given to the child, or likely to be given to him, if an order were not made, not being what it would be reasonable to expect a parent to give or the child being beyond parental control.

The threshold criteria for care and supervision are measured objectively against a reasonable standard of parenting (Box 22.9). Harm is defined as the impairment of the child's health or development. The question of whether the harm is of sufficient degree to be considered "significant" is measured by comparison with "that which could reasonably be expected of a similar child."

Interim care/supervision orders (ICO)/(ISO)

Interim orders may last for an initial period of up to eight weeks, followed by extensions of up to four weeks at a time. The court is anxious to avoid delay and will be unhappy about continued extensions without good reason. Directions may be given on the making of an interim order about contact with family and others and medical or psychiatric assessment.

Box 22.9 **Definition of terms in the Children Act**

- Harm – Ill-treatment or the impairment of health and development [including for example, impairment suffered from seeing or hearing the ill-treatment of another]
- Development – Physical, intellectual, social, emotional, or behavioural development.
- Health – Physical or mental health
- Ill-treatment – Forms of ill-treatment that are not physical; includes sexual and emotional abuse

Directions for medical and psychiatric examination and assessment

The court has power to order, control, or forbid medical and psychiatric examinations and assessments when making interim orders. The directions may cover who is to carry out the assessment, the venue, those accompanying the child, and disclosure of results. As discussed earlier in emergency protection orders, the child may make an informed decision to refuse, in which case the advice and help of the Children's Guardian should be sought and the matter should be referred back to the court.

Child assessment orders

Child assessment orders (CAO) are intended for situations when a local authority has access to a child but where there is a lack of cooperation in allowing an assessment to take place. If the child is thought to be at risk of considerable harm but in no immediate danger that would require removal or retention in a safe place (for example, a long term, ongoing situation requiring further assessment), then this order may assist. The local authority must give notice to allow parties to make arrangements to attend. The court would have to be satisfied of the risk to the child and the need for the order and to be informed of previous unproductive attempts to negotiate with the family. The order may last up to seven days, during which the child may go away from home but this should be only when absolutely necessary for the assessment to take place. On hearing an application for a child assessment order the court may decide, when necessary, to make an emergency protection order instead.

Private law orders

Private law orders are proceedings designated by section 8(3)-(4) of the act as "family proceedings" within which the court has power to make a wide range of orders. Some of these, including family assistance orders and those colloquially referred to as "section 8 orders" (residence, contact, specific issue, and prohibited steps), may be made by the court of its own volition. Some people are entitled to apply for these orders; others need leave. The criteria for leave focus on the welfare and needs of the child. Special restrictions apply to applications by local authority foster parents. The section 8 orders most used are briefly outlined below.

Residence

"An order settling the arrangements to be made as to the person with whom a child is to live." The order attaches to a person not a place. Residence may be shared – for example, to the mother during term time and to the father in the school holidays. Parental responsibility may be granted, with a residence order, to those who do not otherwise have it, and this will exist along with the order. There are special provisions for birth fathers. Anyone with a residence order in their favour may take the child out of the country for up to one month for holiday purposes. Otherwise, when there is a residence order, removal of the child from the country or a change of surname will require the written consent of all those with parental responsibility or leave of the court.

Contact

"An order requiring the person with whom a child lives or is to live, to allow the child to visit or stay with the person named in the order, or for the child and that person to have contact with each other." Contact includes telephone calls, tape and video recordings, letters, parcels, and any other form of communication.

There is a different contact order available to regulate contact with a child in statutory care, which has its own special provisions.

Specific issue

"An order giving directions for the purpose of determining a question which has arisen, or which may arise, in connection with any aspect of parental responsibility for a child," section 8. This order is designed to resolve disputes between those with the power to make decisions in a child's life and who cannot resolve their disagreements by negotiation. A local authority, or anyone with leave of the court, may use this provision to seek a ruling from the court on issues such as medical treatment. Application for specific issue to the High Court could be used, for example, when those with parental responsibility for a young child disagree about a proposed medical treatment that doctors consider necessary in the interests of the child. Local authorities may apply for a specific issue order to obtain a court direction about the medical treatment for a child, but a specific issue order cannot be made in respect of a child who is in care.

Prohibited steps

"An order that no step which could be taken by a parent in meeting his parental responsibility for a child, and which is of a kind specified by the order, shall be taken by any person without the consent of the court." This order operates rather like an injunction and is useful, for example, when a parent is threatening to take a child out of the country without consent. It may be obtained in emergencies without notice. It is not available for a child who is subject to a care order.

Further reading

Cullen D, M Lane. *Child care law: a summary of the law in England and Wales.* London, British Association for Adoption and Fostering, 2003. (A brief overview.)

Department of Health, Home Office and Employment, DoE. *Assessing children in need and their families: practice guidance.* London: The Stationery Office, 2000.

Department of Health, Home Office and Employment, DoE. *Framework for the assessment of children in need and their families.* London: The Stationery Office, 2000.

Department of Health. *Reference guide to consent for examination or treatment.* London: Department of Health, 2001.

Department of Health, Home Office. *Working together to safeguard children.* London: The Stationery Office, 1999. (Revised version issued July 2005, in consultation process).

Department of Health. *What to do if you're worried a child is being abused.* London: DoH, 2003. www.dh.gov.uk/assetRoot/04/06/13/03/04061303.pdf

General Medical Council. *Confidentiality: protecting and providing information.* London: GMC, 2004. www.gmc-uk.org

Hershman D, McFarlane A. *Children law and practice.* Bristol: Family Law. (A comprehensive three volume reference work, regularly updated).

Home Office, Department of Health. *Achieving best evidence in criminal proceedings: guidance for vulnerable or intimidated witnesses, including children.* London: The Stationery Office, 2002.

Butler-Sloss E. *The report of the inquiry into child abuse in Cleveland.* London: HMSO, 1987.

Conventions

UN Convention on the Rights of the Child (in force in the UK on 15 January 1992)

European Convention for the Protection of Human Rights and Fundamental Freedoms

CHAPTER 23

About Courts

Barbara Mitchels

The legislation, procedures, and terminology in this chapter reflect practice in England and Wales. Readers who work elsewhere will recognise the importance, philosophy, and principles of working together with other agencies when they are concerned about child abuse. They should be familiar with equivalent legislation procedures and terminology used in their country of practice

There are two types of court case. The first is criminal proceedings, in which a criminal prosecution is brought against a person accused of a criminal offence. They may admit the offence, defend it, or let the prosecution prove the case. The second is civil proceedings, in which one person makes a claim against another, often for financial compensation and/or a judicial remedy, such as an injunction, for breach of a civil right or duty, or for an action that has caused some kind of loss or damage. The problems that arise within domestic life, for example domestic violence or child abuse, may involve prosecu-

tions in the criminal courts running concurrently with proceedings in the Family Courts. The Children Act 1989 defines "family proceedings" to include care and supervision applications, and creates a 'menu' of orders which are available to the court. See Chapter 22 for further details.

Various courts may require evidence from doctors (Box 23.1). Sometimes doctors are expert witnesses in the criminal prosecution of alleged offenders and, occasionally, in civil proceedings. A common role for doctors is in child protection proceedings under the Children Act 1989. Many of the child protection referrals to social services prove to be unfounded, others are resolved through cooperation between social services and the family concerned to meet the needs of the child. Only a small proportion result in criminal prosecutions or in child protection proceedings.

The criminal and civil justice systems operate differently. In criminal cases, because a person's reputation and liberty may be at stake if they are convicted, the rules of evidence are strict, and it is the task of the prosecution to prove the case against the accused "beyond reasonable doubt." The court requires the "best evidence" and so will not permit certain types of evidence in hearing the case. The civil courts have a less strict standard of proof – the "balance of probabilities" – in which the court has to be satisfied that the facts alleged are "more likely than not" to have occurred. In cases where child

Figure 23.1 Royal Court of Justice, London.

Box 23.1 **Order of evidence in contested cases**

Criminal cases
- Prosecution opens case
- Prosecution witnesses
- Defence witnesses
- Closing speech for prosecution (in some cases)
- Closing speech(es) for defence
- Judge sums up
- Jury/magistrates retire for decision

Procedure for each witness
- Evidence in chief
- Cross examination
- Re-examination
- Court (magistrate/judge) questions witness

Child protection proceedings
- Parties introduced to court
- Applicant (usually local authority) opens case
- Applicant's witnesses
- Respondent's witnesses
- Child's evidence (if any)
- Guardian's evidence
- Respondents closing speech
- Guardian's closing speech
- Court retires for decision

abuse is alleged in care proceedings, the strength of the evidence required to establish the facts alleged increases proportionately to the seriousness of the allegations made.

In criminal proceedings, which are adversarial, the objective is to ensure that the accused person has a fair trial with procedural safeguards to protect their rights. Certain evidence – for example, character, or previous convictions – is therefore excluded or restricted.

In contrast, the paramount consideration in child protection proceedings is the welfare of the child, and so all relevant evidence is put before the court to facilitate an informed decision in the child's best interests. Parents may have medical or psychiatric problems that affect their potential parenting ability. The law now requires disclosure in care proceedings of all medical and psychiatric reports, favourable or not. A Children's Guardian is appointed to advise the court in child protection cases and has access to all social work records. The Children's Guardian has no automatic right of access to medical records but may see those of a parent, carer or child with appropriate consent or leave of the court. Documents seen and mentioned in the report of the Children's Guardian are admissible in evidence under the Children Act.

In both criminal and civil cases, witnesses may be ordered to attend court and to bring relevant documents with them, including medical records. Experts should inform the court in advance of their availability, to assist in listing the case.

Criminal prosecutions

The criminal prosecution of adults starts in the Magistrates' Court. Criminal cases against young people under 18 start in the Youth Courts. Serious criminal cases (including trials of young people in certain circumstances) will be committed to the Crown Court for trial. In the Magistrates' Court, three lay (not legally qualified) magistrates or a single, legally qualified stipendiary magistrate, will hear the case, sometimes accompanied by a lay magistrate. Lay magistrates receive any necessary legal advice or guidance from the clerk to the court, who sits in front of them during the hearing and is responsible for taking a note of the evidence. A court usher is responsible for the smooth running of the case, noting names of those present, fetching witnesses from their hiding place in the canteen, carrying confidential papers between the courts and assisting the court generally.

In the Crown Court the case is heard by a judge sitting alone if the defendant is pleading guilty, or by a judge and jury if the matter is contested. The judge has a clerk and a court usher to assist with administrative matters. The Crown Court has a more formal setting, with judge and advocates wearing wigs, gowns, and robes. The accused is likely to be in a dock, possibly guarded. Most Crown Courts now have strong security measures in place.

If an accused person pleads guilty to the offence then, before sentencing, the magistrates or judge will hear evidence in mitigation, which may include probation reports and medical and psychiatric assessments. Evidence in criminal cases is by statement (see Chapter 19) and oral evidence where required. If the matter is contested, evidence will be called in a specific order and the magistrates or the jury are then invited to retire to consider their verdict. The role of the judge is to advise the jury on matters of law, but issues of fact are for the jury to decide. Sentencing is a matter for the magistrates or judge.

Appeals lie from the Magistrates' Court to the Crown Court (where appeals against conviction may be retried) and also to the High Court by way of case stated (that is, without hearing the live evidence again). Appeals from the Crown Court lie to the High Court, the Court of Appeal (Criminal Division), and on a point of law of public importance to the House of Lords.

Child protection cases

The Children Act 1989 created one court comprising three levels with similar powers so that cases may be transferred up or down the levels as appropriate. Child protection cases may be brought in the Magistrates' Family Proceedings Court (FPC) (Fig. 23.3), in the County Court (family division), or in the family division of the High Court. The hearings currently are "in camera," neither press nor visitors being given access, although there are political moves at

Figure 23.2 Combined Court Centre, Leeds.

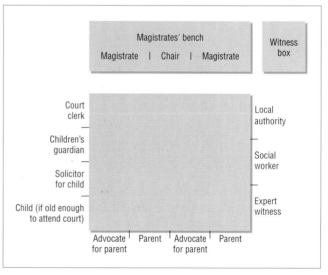

Figure 23.3 Layout of Family Proceedings Court.

the moment to permit greater public access, with safeguards. All the professionals involved in child protection should have a common priority – the welfare of the child.

Appeals lie from the Family Proceedings Court to the High Court, and appeals from cases in the County Court and High Court lie to the Court of Appeal (family division). Appeals on points of law of public importance may go to the House of Lords. Evidence in these cases is by statement, filed with the court, and oral evidence when required by the court or parties. Statements may be agreed and then read in the court. An expert witness need attend court only if specifically requested to do so, usually because an aspect of their statement needs clarification or is in some way disputed.

Court procedure

People entering a court building are likely to be security screened. At court, criminal cases will be listed in a notice in the public area by name and child protection cases are listed by the name of the local authority and the reference number. The ushers are a reliable source of information, and will ask the names of all the advocates and witnesses in each case as they arrive. They will need to know where to find the witnesses when required. Usually there are canteen facilities which make the seemingly interminable waiting time bearable. Switch off pagers and mobiles before entering the courtroom.

Entry into the courtroom can make important impressions. Be calm and unhurried. Try not to go into the witness box laden with coat, umbrella, and several bags. Have notes readily accessible, with markers on essential topics for easy referral, and know where to find the necessary information. Be aware that the judge or others may ask to see the notes (see also Box 23.2).

Rules of evidence

Ordinary witnesses may give evidence only of fact. The court decides who is an expert witness. Qualifications and experience should be cited in reports for court (see Chapter 19). Expert witnesses may give fact and opinion, but must be prepared to justify opinions with cogent evidence, e.g. from experience or research.

Figure 23.4 Royal Court of Justice, London.

Figure 23.5 Going in the right direction.

In criminal cases, because the burden of proof is high, the court wants the "best evidence" possible, and therefore the rules about admissibility of evidence are strict. Evidence about siblings, family history, and other incidents may not be admissible. "Hearsay" evidence is disallowed. This means that witnesses can tell the court only what they experienced for themselves, and not what others have told them in order to prove the truth of the matters stated – for example, a child's examination record might note "Karen said while I examined her on 7 July, 2004 'John grabbed me by the arm and twisted it and then he beat me with his belt and it hurt.'" This statement by the child would not be admissible in evidence at John's trial for criminal assault to prove the fact of assault with a belt. It would be admitted only to prove that Karen was alive and well on 7 July, she was capable of speaking, and that she spoke to the doctor during the examination. Karen would have to tell the court herself what John did. However, the medical evidence could report the examination results showing evidence of torsion, and patterns of bruising and belt marks on the skin, corroborating the child's evidence. Special facilities including video links in court are available in specified circumstances for young or vulnerable witnesses as an alternative to giving evidence in chief in the witness box, but young witnesses still

Box 23.2 **Forms of address in court**

- **My Lord or My Lady**: Court of Appeal, High Court judges or any deputy sitting as a High Court judge; and all judges sitting at the Central Criminal Court (the "Old Bailey")
- **Your Honour**: all circuit or other judges sitting in the Crown Court or the County Court.
- **Sir or Madam**: District judges or Registrars sitting in chambers, and magistrates
- **Your Worship**: less common now but still used to address magistrates

It is customary to stand and bow or incline the head to magistrates or judges when they enter or leave the courtroom. A similar courtesy to the bench or judge is appropriate when you enter or leave a court that is in session

have to be available for cross examination, and this can be a distressing experience for children and vulnerable adults.

In contrast, because the ethos of family proceedings is to have before the court all possible relevant evidence to serve the interests of the child, in civil cases concerning the "upbringing, maintenance or welfare of a child" (which includes child protection), the hearsay rule does not apply. The court regulates its own process and decides the weight to give the evidence before it.

How to present evidence

Notes should be the originals, with any alterations and amendments clearly marked, dated, and signed. Be prepared to explain the alteration. Notes from other colleagues may be included if they form part of a continuous medical record (Box 23.3).

X ray pictures and photographs may be produced as exhibits and duly validated and identified by their maker, or, if they form part of medical records, they may be produced by the responsible health practitioner. Samples and specimens may be produced as exhibits and duly identified by the person responsible for taking them or by the health practitioner.

Computer records may be printed and produced, provided they are properly verified. Research findings, references, etc, may be used in court, but be prepared for cross examination by an advocate who may well question the methodology, research sampling methods, hypotheses, aims, and evaluations, so ensure that any work cited and relied upon is well understood. Bring extra copies to court for the judge and the advocates.

Expert witnesses are independent, no matter who pays their fee. Though they may be instructed and called to court by a particular party, their duty is to be objective and to serve the court and not that party. Experts may wish to confer with each other, and it is therefore courteous to do so in the presence of their respective instructing advocates, or at least with their knowledge. Experts should demonstrate their independence by non-partisan behaviour. It is wise to consult the instructing lawyer first about any request to confer with another party or witness. During an adjournment – for example, for lunch – the court does not permit discussion by anyone with a witness when they are still in the process of giving evidence.

Ordinary witnesses have to wait outside the courtroom to prevent them being influenced by hearing what others say. In family courts, expert witnesses can sit in and hear all the evidence to help them to formulate an opinion on the basis of all available information. Sit near the instructing advocate if possible – they may need an expert's help as the case progresses. Silence is observed in the court while in session – audible asides or critical comment of other witnesses is highly unprofessional. If you need to communicate urgently with the advocate, you can pass a note or whisper if the comment is short. If a longer consultation is necessary, the advocate may seek a short adjournment.

In the witness box, after the oath or affirmation, it is courteous to remain standing until invited to sit. Behave with dignity, and no matter how irritating or irrelevant the questions seem to be, remain calm and courteous. The qualities of carefulness, openness, impartiality, knowledge, confidence, and trustworthiness are as impor-

Box 23.3 **Notes and records**

Advocates and others may ask to see case notes and records. Disclosure of these is a matter for the court to decide. Therefore if in doubt seek directions from the judge or magistrate

tant for effective witnesses as they are for good clinicians. Do not venture opinions on topics unless they can be justified. In criminal trials, expert witnesses may have to tolerate anger, sarcasm, and even obtuseness from advocates, but resist the urge to respond with defensiveness or a show of skill. Sometimes advocates try to interrupt a witness mid-way through making a point. It is difficult for an advocate to interrupt a witness who is speaking directly to the judge. Listen to the question, then turn to face the magistrates or judge and direct the answers to them, rather than to the advocate who asked the question. This then makes it much more difficult for the advocate to interrupt you whilst answering. If you are interrupted before saying all you want, say so, and return to the unfinished point before answering the next question. If you have found a question difficult to follow, ask counsel to repeat the question rather than attempt to answer it.

Advocates may ask questions that appear to be the result of relevant research but may well be just playing with words, or explorations. Treat this like a viva in an examination, and take such questions calmly, take time to consider the point then reply to the question asked, preferably without adding further unsolicited information, unless it is relevant and vital to the case.

Speak clearly and slowly enough for the judge and others to take notes of points they need to record. Do not rush evidence; take time to think before answering questions. Be prepared to refer to notes or medical records before answering. Be accurate and concise. If the answer is not known or unclear, do not be afraid to say so.

Cross examination provides an opportunity to reconsider, correct or modify previous evidence. Be ready to concede points made by counsel if they are a reasonable interpretation of the facts.

Remember that in criminal cases the jury may have to rely on what they hear in court.

Witnesses should not leave the court building until the court has given consent for release. Make a habit of asking for the court's consent to be released at the end of giving evidence. Try to make a calm exit, picking up notes efficiently, and leaving with dignity.

Bring a diary; if the case is adjourned it is helpful to know dates available for future hearings. Courts are usually considerate of doctors' clinical commitments and try to assist by calling evidence at convenient times.

Expenses

Expenses of travel, accommodation, and time spent in travelling and at court should be the responsibility of the party calling the witness, with the fee scales and limits agreed in advance. If the report and evidence is publicly funded, the instructing solicitor should ensure that the expenditure is authorised in advance by the Legal Services Commission and this should be confirmed in writing to the expert witness.

Further reading

Barskey AE, Gould JW. *Clinicians in court: a guide.* New York: Guilford Press, 2002

Bond T, Sandhu, A. (2005) The Therapist in Court. London, BACP and Sage.

Brodsky SL. *Coping with cross-examination: and other pathways to effective testimony.* Washington, DC: American Psychological Association, 2004.

Home Office, Department of Health. *Achieving best evidence in criminal proceedings: guidance for vulnerable or intimidated witnesses, including children.* London: Stationery Office, 2002.

Wall N. *Expert witnesses in Children Act cases.* Bristol: Family Law. Jordan Publishing, 2000.

CHAPTER 24

Dilemmas

Roy Meadow

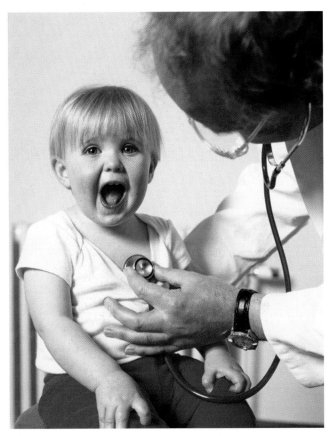

Figure 24.1 Paediatrics is usually happy work. With permission from Tek Image/Science Photo Library. Posed by model.

Child abuse runs counter to the views that most of us have of family life – the reciprocity of love between parent and child and our belief that children fare best in their own homes with their own parents. We wish that child abuse did not happen, therefore diagnosing and reporting child abuse is distasteful. Clinicians are familiar with the happiness and satisfaction at identifying the cause of serious or puzzling symptoms; diagnosis opens the way for help and healing (Fig. 24.1). When the diagnosis is child abuse, those feelings are replaced by sadness, worry, horror, and, sometimes, feelings of impotence or betrayal. Diagnosing or reporting abuse disrupts the usual trust between the child's parent and the doctor, and forces the doctor into an alien world of criminal processes. There are no thanks for diagnosing

child abuse. The medical practitioner who suggests the possibility may incur abuse and aggravation from the family, adverse publicity, and considerable disruption to a planned work schedule because of attendance at case discussions, case conferences, and courts (Fig. 24.2); as well as much extra paperwork writing reports. For most doctors there will therefore be a tendency to under-diagnose and to under-report abuse rather than the reverse.

Confidentiality

Even for paediatricians and child psychiatrists, whose priority is the child, reporting abuse is difficult; it is more difficult for general practitioners, psychiatrists, and other specialists whose patient is the perpetrator and who may feel that they are breaching confidences. There is understandable concern about whether to inform statutory agencies of abuse and how much information to divulge at multi-agency child protection case conferences. Nevertheless, the professional and legal position is clear. The advice on medical confidentiality from the General Medical Council, the British Medical Association, and the Academy of Medical Royal Colleges is that the needs of the child must take priority (Box 24.1). That enables appropriate reporting of concern. It also permits non-disclosure of information about a child under the age of 16 to his or her parents, if it is not in the interests of the child.

The requirement in relation to providing information for reviews of serious cases of abuse (Part 8 Reviews) is similar (Box 24.2). The doctor should respond to requests for information; if in exceptional circumstances he or she believes there is a good reason not to dis-

---

Box 24.1 **Guidance from the General Medical Council***

"If you believe a patient to be a victim of neglect or physical, sexual or emotional abuse and that the patient cannot give or withhold consent to disclosure, you must give information promptly to an appropriate responsible person or statutory agency, where you believe that the disclosure is in the patient's best interests. If, for any reason you believe that disclosure of information is not in the best interests of an abused or neglected patient, you should discuss the issues with an experienced colleague. If you decide not to disclose information, you must be prepared to justify your decision."

Confidentiality: protecting and providing information. London: GMC, 2004

close information, the doctor is advised to note the circumstances and be prepared to explain the decision to the authorities.

Box 24.2 **Case reviews**

Case reviews are set up to identify why a child has incurred severe or fatal harm. In England and Wales, subject to the Children Act 1989, they are referred to as *Part 8 Reviews*. These reviews try to identify why a child was seriously harmed, the purpose being to protect other children.

Threshold for reporting

The courts have clear direction, in the statutes, for the "threshold criteria" that should be satisfied before a care or supervision order is made. Doctors do not have uniformly clear direction in threshold criteria for reporting suspicions of abuse. Within the UK there are different thresholds. In England and Wales, paediatricians are advised that the threshold for reporting is "a reasonable belief that there is a real risk of significant harm"; in Scotland it is belief or suspicion that a child is being abused or is at risk. Within any one country, however, a doctor may have variable and sometimes conflicting advice. The General Medical Council stipulates belief of serious harm, yet many doctors have local guidelines saying, "Even if there is only a suspicion of significant harm, a referral should be made to social services and/or the police." Such advice is easier to give than to follow.

In many cases of child abuse the medical assessment contributes little or nothing; in others it is the major factor influencing social and legal procedures. That knowledge weighs heavily on the mind of the reporting doctor.

Though it is easy to state that any suspected child abuse should be reported, experienced professionals think carefully before so doing. They worry that their suspicion may be unfounded and that investigation of their suspicion may be counterproductive and not in the child's best interests. The worries about reporting at too low a threshold are understandable because of awareness of the great upset that investigation of suspected child abuse might cause for the family. They may also have doubts about the efficacy of the child protection procedures, which sometimes are criticised for putting more resources into the investigation of an allegation than to the provision of help for a family in difficulty. They may have seen the practical difficulty of helping children whose protection is at issue, who invariably have multiple needs, many of which cannot be met. (One third come from lone parent families; nearly half live in a home that lacks a wage earner; domestic violence, substance misuse, and mental illness are common.) They may also have doubts about

(b)

(a)   (c)

Figure 24.2 (a)–(c) Working with legal council and testifying in court is a necessary part of child protection work.

the ability of the agencies to protect children and of the benefit of alternative parenting, should that be necessary.

The publicity given to children removed needlessly from their own homes is misleading: in over 95% of cases children stay at home, and of those who are removed from parental care, over two thirds are returned within the next six months. Substitute care is open to criticism. About 5% of children in care are eventually adopted, and, though placement of infants for adoption has an excellent outcome, it is more problematic for older children. In relation to fostering, infants fare well and young children and older teenagers do reasonably well, but for those in middle childhood there is a considerable chance of the fostering relationship breaking down. That sort of knowledge, plus the publicity given to child abuse taking place in substitute care, gives those reluctant to notify abuse an extra excuse for their inaction.

Sometimes, hopefully rarely, the diagnosis may be made inappropriately. As long as the doctor's actions were reasonable and in accordance with national and local guidelines, feelings of guilt about harming a child or family should be lessened. All doctors make errors in diagnosis. Moreover, it is important to differentiate between the diagnostic process and subsequent management. Child abuse is common, therefore consideration of abuse as a possible reason for many childhood conditions, and including it in the list of differential diagnoses, is a necessary part of everyday practice; doing so should lead to appropriate investigation (Figs 24.3–24.7).

For many doctors who suspect abuse, referral to a local paediatrician transfers the clinical problem. For that paediatrician, however, the problems begin. Some tasks are relatively easy – checking the child protection register, telephoning the health visitor and general practitioner, meeting other relatives, and consulting colleagues. Others are more difficult because it is neither as easy for the doctor, nor as acceptable for the parents, to arrange for a social work assessment as it is to arrange for the child to have computed tomography or be referred to an ear, nose, and throat specialist.

Thresholds for clinical action vary according to the consequent risks. Doctors readily prescribe antibiotics and arrange blood tests for suspected infection because the potential risk of those actions is small compared with the possible benefit. They are less ready

Figure 24.3 "He hit the edge of the chair" – or did someone hit him?

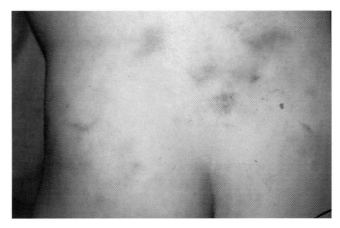

Figure 24.4 "The two of them were playing together" – or was there sexual abuse?

to arrange invasive, potentially dangerous investigations or treatments. In these familiar clinical circumstances the doctor adjusts the threshold for action on sure knowledge of the risks. With suspected abuse the doctor is in unsure territory. He or she has no measure of the potential disruption to a family resulting from social services assessment and subsequent investigation for possible abuse.

Action relates to the probability of correct diagnosis. In current parlance lay people use "clinical" as an adjective to describe something that is particularly certain, neat, efficient, and effective. Clinicians know different; they are aware of the uncertainties of their work and that the art of clinical medicine is to take, and follow, firm decisions on the basis of inconclusive evidence, and then to amend their diagnosis and management according to progress and further information. Therefore doctors liasing with child protection agencies or providing court testimony need to clarify the nature or uncertainty of their work.

Uncertainty is lessened by discussion with colleagues. Difficult or potentially disastrous diagnoses benefit from wider consultation. Additional opinions from experienced generalists and specialist colleagues will add to the views of the doctor with special experience of child abuse. Clinicians should bear in mind that their medical diagnosis is merely one of several professional opinions contributing to the conclusion that the child has or has not been abused

The uncertain threshold for reporting places UK doctors in a difficult position with their regulatory authority. They are expected to report suspected abuse but it is not mandatory, so there is no legally defined threshold. Moreover there is no automatic presumption, as there is in the Republic of Ireland, that the doctor who reports abuse will have done so in good faith. Currently UK doctors are in the anomalous position of being reported to their regulatory body for failing to report abuse, as well as for reporting abuse. The latter complaint, usually from the child's relatives, is the more common.

The priority is to act in the child's best interests, and, though individual doctors may have varying thresholds for diagnosis and notification, early collaboration with social services is likely to achieve a more uniform approach countrywide that serves children and their parents best. Such early collaboration is more likely when social services adopt a careful and sensitive approach to their investiga-

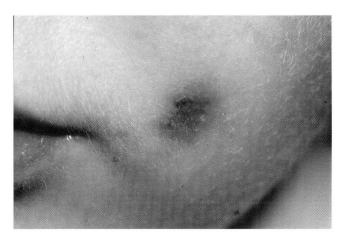

Figure 24.5 "He was stung" – or deliberately burned?

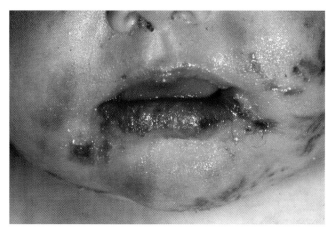

Figure 24.6 "She fell into her feeding bowl" – or was she pushed?

tion, avoiding hasty decisions or intemperate separation of children from their parents.

Who should examine the child?

A doctor may be reluctant to be involved in child abuse and slow to take on the responsibility of examining a child for signs of abuse. Most reasons are linked to either lack of training or lack of appropriate support and multidisciplinary help. A common fear of an inexperienced doctor is that he or she may jeopardise, by their interview and examination, a subsequent investigation that may be required by social services or the police.

Doctors should be reassured about their role and have clear priorities. Their chief duty is to the child and to the child's immediate wellbeing. Thus, if the child is in danger, is in pain, or requires resuscitation or special investigation, get on with it, just as is the case with any other child in trouble. Appropriate medical investigation and treatment must take priority. Further assessment and forensic tests are a secondary consideration; important, but less important than the child's immediate safety and wellbeing. Most doctors will have access to local guidelines about what to do if they suspect or diagnose abuse. These should be followed. In the UK there will be consultant paediatricians and forensic physicians on call who are

experienced in child abuse work, and there should be a duty social worker available (Box 24.3).

Most child abuse is not an emergency, and, in those circumstances, it is important to proceed cautiously and to ensure that examinations and assessments are performed in the best way. The checklist provided by the Royal College of Paediatrics and Child Health is helpful.

False allegations

Many allegations of abuse by parents do not lead to further proceedings or are unsubstantiated after investigation. Some are unsubstantiated because there is insufficient evidence for further action. But in other cases the allegations may be false.

False allegations of abuse, particularly sexual abuse, are common at the time of parental separation and disputes concerning custody of, or access to, children. In the US it is reported that at least one third of the allegations of abuse that are made in the context of custody disputes are false. Many others are undetermined. The usual circumstance is the child's mother alleging sexual abuse by the father. The context is difficult because in some cases abuse may have been the reason for separation, and in others, separation has provided the setting for abuse. Moreover, children who did not disclose abuse

---

Box 24.3 **Checklist to consider before examining a child when abuse is suspected**

- Am I the right person to examine the child?
- Are there forensic implications?
- What other doctors/facilities need to be alerted to advise/support?
- Do I know how to contact them?
- Is all relevant health information available?
- Is the issue of consent clarified?
- Has the issue of confidentiality been dealt with?
- Is this the best time for the *child* to undergo the examination?
- Is the environment appropriate – is it child friendly, is privacy ensured?
- Are the right people available to support the child?

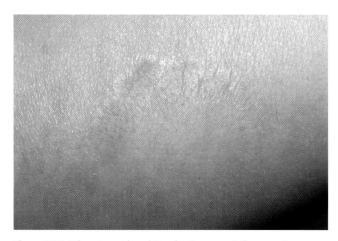

Figure 24.7 "The cat must have bitten her" – or was it the parent?

before their parents separated may feel able to do so when they are living away from the perpetrator; the child's ambivalence and reticence, from fear of doing more harm than good, has then lessened. Nevertheless, amid the unhappiness, bitterness, and selfishness that is sometimes evident when parents separate, false allegations are relatively common and mothers may use an allegation of abuse as a way of preventing the father having access to his children. During the protracted investigation of such cases it is common for children to be denied access to one of their parents, usually the father, for many months or even years; then the child does incur abuse – severe emotional abuse.

Unfounded allegations may come from relatives, neighbours, teachers, and other professionals, but usually they will have been made in a well intentioned, rather than self-serving, way.

Some children give false stories of being abused. The time when a child's testimony was regarded as the absolute truth is past. It is acknowledged that young children are vulnerable to suggestion and will elaborate on misunderstood stories originating from adults and that school children repeat stories that they have learnt from videos. Older children and adolescents may produce an over-detailed story with extravagant, horrific, or erotic detail. For all witnesses recollection of events is altered by the passage of time, misunderstandings, outside pressure, and sometimes intent, resulting in allegations that are untrue. Therefore, there is always more doubt about allegations that are made long after the event, those that lack intimate details and vivid experience or feeling, those without corroborative evidence, and those occurring within the context of parental disputes about custody or contact. The assessment of such testimony requires an experienced and skilled person who has a non-judgmental and open mind in relation to the accusation and the skill to elicit reliable information without reinforcing false elements by repeated questions or suggestions.

Further reading

Department of Health. *Child protection: messages from research*. London: HMSO, 1995.

Heiman ML. Putting the puzzle together: validating allegations of child sexual abuse. *J Child Psychol Psychiatry* 1992;33:311–29.

NSPCC. *Listening to children*. London: Longmans, 1990.

Craft AW, Hall DMB. Munchausen syndrome by proxy and sudden infant death. *BMJ* 2004;328:1309–12.

General Medical Council. *Confidentiality: protecting and providing information*. London: GMC, 2004. www.gmc-uk.org/guidance/archive/library/confidentiality_faq.asp

Royal College of Paediatricians and Child Health. *Responsibilities of doctors in child protection cases with regard to confidentiality*. London: RCPCH, 2004.

Index